CATHOLICISM, COMMUNISM, & CRIMINAL REFORMATION

By
David H. Lukenbill

A Chulu Press Book

Chulu Press First Edition published 2013

IBSN: 978-0-9892429-0-5

Copyright © 2013 by David H. Lukenbill
ALL RIGHTS RESERVED
PRINTED IN THE UNITED STATES OF AMERICA
First Edition

Published by The Lampstand Foundation

www.lampstandfoundation.org

We glorify God to attract others to Him

For Marlene & Erika Always

Contents

Preface: 9

Introduction: 13

Communism in Russia 43

Communism in America: 59

Communism & Fatima: 117

Conclusion: 133

Afterword: 159

References: 169

About the Author: 181

Prayer for Prisoners: 183

Prayer to St. Dismas: 185

Prayer to St. Michael: 187

Preface

This is the eighth book in our annual book publication schedule, which, along with our annual policy papers, forms the foundation of our apostolate work.

As my ultimate audience, beyond the members of the Lampstand Foundation, is penitential criminals, many of whom are in prison, my books are written by marshaling various resources through copious quotes to help make the points I am attempting to get across; and these resources are as important for my penitential criminal audience to access as the work of our apostolate.

In prison, reading a book whose ideas were being presented which were subtle and not easily understood, cutting against the grain of normative narrative, in books that were largely narrative with few references; would always elicit from me the same response, how does the author know that; and with no access to academic libraries to seek out support of the position taken, I could easily discount it as one author's opinion.

I use a lot of references to show support for these ideas and for those readers in prison who have little access to research.

There is a massive library of words about the Catholic Church and its teaching stretching back two millennia and while much of it is pure gold, much is also pure dross.

I try to find the gold—as I define it—and pass it on to you dear reader, for we are encumbered by too much dross already in the world and in the world of ideas and books, it is hard to find clear support of the eternal Catholic teaching, especially among modern Catholic writers as all too many are caught up in dissent, and are corrupting the teaching rather than validating it.

Many of my references, as you will discover, are from old books, books written in the early and mid-part of the last century, which is one of the clearer moments of clarity within the Catholic world.

The lens I filter all things Catholic through, is that of the two Universal Catechisms, from Trent and Vatican II, the Four Constitutions of Vatican II—as the most recent dogmatic documents from the most recent ecumenical council—the papal magisterium, and the Angelic Doctor, St. Thomas Aquinas.

The edition I am now using of the Four Constitutions: *Sacrosanctum Concilium: The Sacred Liturgy*; *Lumen Gentium: On the Church*; *Dei Verbum: The Word of God*; *Gaudium et Specs: The Church in the Modern World*; is from the book: *The Second Vatican Council: The Four Constitutions*, published in 2013—the 50th anniversary of the opening of the council—by Ignatius Press, San Francisco, with translations by the Catholic Truth Society, London, which is the United Kingdom publisher to the Holy See.

Translations are important as all documents of the Church are published in Latin and ensuring the translation from Latin to English hews as closely to what was intended is crucial. What I look for is the connection to the translations by conservative Catholic leaders and in the case of the book I prefer, the four leaders—Cardinal Francis Arinze, Cardinal Paul Poupard, Cardinal Angelo Scola, and Archbishop Charles Chaput—who've written introductions to the four constitutions are all considered as such.

And I would be remiss if I did not speak to how I write my books, which is, entirely alone. I do all of my own editing and self-publish through Create Space, the very fine self-publishing vehicle of Amazon.

Each book is written over the period of a year, with, lately, the first outline being the Annual St. Dismas Feast Day Policy Primer on March 25th for members of the Lampstand Foundation; then expanded for publication as Lampstand's annual book—also free to members—in December.

Introduction

What is important—in the context of our apostolate work through The Lampstand Foundation—is not the theory of Communism, "to each according to need", which many may support; but the influence on criminals from the system of government and its practice under Lenin and Stalin in Russia, Mao in China, and the lessor monsters of our world; practice continuing largely unchanged today except as modified within the constrictions created by the ability of global communications about governmental atrocities making it much more difficult to keep such atrocities hidden now than during the last century; and a governing practice diametrically opposed to the sacred doctrine of the Catholic Church, who Communism sees as its most dangerous enemy.

Communism—in addition to the countries under its capture—is experiencing resurgence among young leftists, as Goldberg (2013) writes:

> *For those too young to remember the Cold War but old enough to be trapped by the Great Recession, Marxism holds new appeal…*
>
> It's too simple to say that Marxism is back, because it never truly went away. In the United States after the fall of the Berlin Wall, though, it was largely confined to university English departments, becoming the stuff of abstruse, inward-looking and jargon-choked cultural critique. Then came the economic crash, Occupy Wall Street, and the ongoing disaster of austerity in Europe. "Around the time of Occupy in particular, a lot of different kinds of lefties, working at mainstream or literary publications, sort of found each other, started

talking to each other, and found out who was most interested in class politics," says Sarah Leonard, the 25-year-old associate editor of Dissent, the social-democratic journal founded almost 60 years ago by Irving Howe. "We have essentially found an old politics that makes sense now."

In the United States, of course, Marxism remains an intellectual current rather than a mass movement. Certainly, millennials are famously progressive; a much-discussed 2011 Pew poll found that 49 percent of people between 18 and 29 had a favorable view of socialism, while only 46 percent felt positively about capitalism. It's hard to say exactly what this means—it's not as if young people are sending Das Kapital racing up the best-seller lists or reconstituting communist cells. Still, it's been decades since so many young thinkers have been so engaged in imagining a social order not governed by the imperatives of the market. (n.p.)

Encouraging this revival is a new venture by radical publishers Verso, publications called Pocket Communism, offering several new books on the emergence of the new interest in Communism, which can be seen at http://www.versobooks.com/series_collections/11-pocket-communism

Getting our mind wrapped around this historical atheistic evil requires a journey through the virtual hurricane of words used to describe it and another point: Communism is rarely believed in by the leaders of Communist countries as they are totalitarians and their operating narrative is power; but Communism is used as the operating narrative—virtually a faith system, though atheistic—for the people to believe in; important to keep in mind as we wend our way through the intersection of the Church, Communism and Fatima.

The seminal Russian Christian philosopher Berdyaev (1960) describes the operating narrative:

> The really important thing is that now the Russian communists represent the government. The State is in their hands, and this State belongs to the period of dictatorship, a dictatorship of world view, a dictatorship which is not only political and economic but also intellectual, a dictatorship over spirit, conscience and thought. This dictatorship makes no bones about the mean it employs; it employs all means. This state of affairs is an ideocracy; it is one of the transformations of the platonic Utopia. It is this which makes the denial of freedom of conscience and thought inevitable, and makes inevitable religious persecution. All controversies in the sphere of theory, ideas and philosophy, and all disputes in the practical, political and economic world in Soviet Russia, are fought out under the banners of orthodoxy and heresy. All those who incline to the 'right' or to the 'left' in philosophy or in politics are regarded as inclined to heresy; and the exposure of heretics and the persecution of those convicted of heresy is continually taking place. But the distinction between orthodoxy and heresy is a religious, a theological distinction, it is not philosophical and political. When politics are placed under the banner of an orthodoxy, then the State is regarded as a Church, and persecution on the ground of faith and opinion cannot be avoided. Christian theocracy in the Middle Ages was like this, and so is the Soviet communist 'theocracy', so is Hitler's Third Reich, and so is every state which professes to be totalitarian. I have already said that Ivan the Terrible, the most notable exponent of the theory of autocracy, founded the conception of an Orthodox Tsardom in which the salvation of the souls of his subjects was one of the duties of the Tsar. The functions of the Church are transferred to the State.

> The communist government also is concerned for the salvation of the souls of its subjects; it desires to bring them up in the one saving truth; it knows the truth, the truth of dialectic materialism. The communist government, which is an unlimited government, finds its motive power in hatred of Christianity, in which it sees the cause of slavery, exploitation and darkness of mind. (pp. 168-169)

Communism is one of the most malevolent manifestations of Modernism as defined by Hardon (1999):

> According to Modernism, religion is essentially a matter of experience, personal and collective. There is no objective revelation from God to the human race, on which Christianity is finally based, nor any reasonable grounds for credibility in the Christian faith, based on miracles or the testimony of history. Faith, therefore, is uniquely from within. In fact it is part of human nature, "a kind of motion of the heart," hidden and unconscious. It is, in Modernist terms, a natural instinct belonging to the emotions, a "feeling for the divine" that cannot be expressed in words or doctrinal propositions, an attitude of spirit that all people have naturally but that some are more aware of having. Modernism was condemned by Pope St. Pius X in two formal documents, *Lamentabili* and *Pascendi*, both published in 1907. (p. 356)

Belloc (1938) describes the "Modern Attack" of which Communism is an aspect:

> Communism (which is only one manifestation, and probably a passing one, of this Modern Attack) professes to be directed towards a certain good, to wit, the abolition of poverty. But it does not tell you why this should be a good; it does not admit that its scheme is also to destroy other things which are

> also by the common consent of mankind good...(p. 147)

> The Modern Attack on the Catholic Church, the most universal that she has suffered since her foundation, has so far progressed that it has already produced social, intellectual and moral forms which combined give it the savor of a religion...(*Ibid.* p. 148)

> Now Communism is full slavery. It is the modern enemy working openly, undisguisedly, and at high pressure. Communism denies God, denies the dignity and therefor the freedom of the human soul, and openly enslaves men to what it calls "the State"—but what is in practice a body of favored officials. (*Ibid.* p. 151)

The leaders of Communist countries, as we now well know from the research and revelations over the past several decades, do not always believe in Communist principles, and we see this in the great wealth they take for themselves while leaving little for the people, and here a great contrast with the Church, whose leaders still remain largely poor, committed to their oath of poverty and chastity.

During the Ecumenical Council of Vatican II, once an agreement was reached between the Vatican and Russia not to mention Communism—which we will explore at some length later—the Church used the term "Modern atheism", as proclaimed in the *Pastoral Constitution on the Modern World: Gaudium et Specs:*

> 20. Modern atheism often takes on a systematic expression which, in addition to other causes, stretches the desires for human independence to such a point that it poses difficulties against any kind of dependence on God. Those who profess atheism of this sort maintain that it gives man freedom to be an end unto himself, the sole artisan

and creator of his own history. They claim that this freedom cannot be reconciled with the affirmation of a Lord Who is author and purpose of all things, or at least that this freedom makes such an affirmation altogether superfluous. Favoring this doctrine can be the sense of power which modern technical progress generates in man.

Not to be overlooked among the forms of modern atheism is that which anticipates the liberation of man especially through his economic and social emancipation. This form argues that by its nature religion thwarts this liberation by arousing man's hope for a deceptive future life, thereby diverting him from the constructing of the earthly city. Consequently when the proponents of this doctrine gain governmental power they vigorously fight against religion, and promote atheism by using, especially in the education of youth, those means of pressure which public power has at its disposal. (GS, #20, Pope Paul VI, 1965))

In the *Catechism of the Catholic Church* (1997), which emanated from Vatican II, it was also addressed as Atheism:

Atheism

2123 "Many . . . of our contemporaries either do not at all perceive, or explicitly reject, this intimate and vital bond of man to God. Atheism must therefore be regarded as one of the most serious problems of our time."

2124 The name "atheism" covers many very different phenomena. One common form is the practical materialism which restricts its needs and aspirations to space and time. Atheistic humanism falsely considers man to be "an end to himself, and the sole maker, with supreme control, of his own history." Another form of contemporary atheism looks for the liberation of man through economic and social liberation. "It holds that religion, of its very nature, thwarts such emancipation by raising man's hopes in a future life, thus both deceiving him and discouraging him from working for a better form of life on earth."

2125 Since it rejects or denies the existence of God, atheism is a sin against the virtue of religion. The imputability of this offense can be significantly diminished in virtue of the intentions and the circumstances. "Believers can have more than a little to do with the rise of atheism. To the extent that they are careless about their instruction in the faith, or present its teaching falsely, or even fail in their religious, moral, or social life, they must be said to conceal rather than to reveal the true nature of God and of religion."

2126 Atheism is often based on a false conception of human autonomy, exaggerated to the point of refusing any dependence on God. Yet, "to acknowledge God is in no way to oppose the dignity of man, since such dignity is grounded and brought to perfection in God. . . . " "For the Church knows full well that her message is in harmony with the most secret desires of the human heart." (Retrieved August 20, 2013 from http://www.vatican.va/archive/ccc_css/archive/catechism/p3s2c1a1.htm#I)

Communist practice over the last century and continuing today, of using violence and the threat of violence as the primary tool of control, while suppressing freedom of speech and religion, and having its agents infiltrating within those institutions, are the evil markers of totalitarian states everywhere; markers most adeptly developed by Russian Communism; markers representing the tyrannical reality becoming widespread, which is why Our Lady of Fatima warned us about Russia in 1917.

The worldly effectiveness of the practice of using violence and the threat of violence is something professional criminals understand and accept as a central aspect of the criminal/carceral world and any evangelization directed towards professional criminals—defined as those who commit crimes for money excluding pedophiles, rapists, informants, and the insane—that is not congruent with the traditional, pre-conciliar history of Catholicism's response to the evil of Communist totalitarianism will not gain deep and long-lasting traction.

A Church that speaks loudly against evil but does little or nothing in its daily practice to confront it will be seen as a religion that does not walk the talk, a fatal characteristic within the criminal/carceral world.

An example: Bishops who proclaim abortion the great evil it is but allow public leaders and politicians in their diocese, to continually proclaim support for abortion and enlist the public in that support, to escape the sanction of ex-communication for scandal, are those bishops spoken of by the ancients, "The floor of hell is paved with the skulls of bishops."

We desperately need Church shepherds who understand the ongoing threat of the ideas spawned by Communism, such as that recently expressed by Cardinal Burke in relation to the liturgy in an interview with Pentin (2013):

> ZENIT: Some argue the liturgy is mostly about aesthetics, and not as important as, say, good works done in faith. What is your view of this argument that one often hears?
>
> Cardinal Burke: It's a Communist misconception. First of all, the liturgy is about Christ. It's Christ alive in his Church, the glorious Christ coming into

our midst and acting on our behalf through sacramental signs to give us the gift of eternal life to save us. It is the source of any truly charitable works we do, any good works we do. So the person whose heart is filled with charity wants to do good works will, like Mother Teresa, give his first intention to the worship of God so that when he goes to offer charity to a poor person or someone in need, it would be at the level of God Himself, and not some human level.

The Communist misconception is that nothing is about transcendence, everything is about the earthly world. There is no God, there is only man. And the most effective promulgator of this atheistic ideology over the past century has been Communism.

Sowell (2013) comments on the economic ideology of Communism:

> In the 20th century, the most sweeping vision of the Left — Communism — spread over vast regions of the world and encompassed well over a billion human beings. Of these, millions died of starvation in the Soviet Union under Stalin and tens of millions in China under Mao.
>
> Milder versions of socialism, with central planning of national economies, took root in India and in various European democracies.
>
> If the preconceptions of the Left were correct, central planning by educated elites who had vast amounts of statistical data at their fingertips and expertise readily available, and were backed by the power of government, should have been more successful than market economies where millions of individuals pursued their own individual interests willy-nilly.

> But, by the end of the 20th century, even socialist and communist governments began abandoning central planning and allowing more market competition. Yet this quiet capitulation to inescapable realities did not end the noisy claims of the Left. (n.p.)

Fr. Charles (1982) explains Marxist economic analysis:

> The starting point of the Marxist economic analysis was the labour theory of value, a concept inherited by the classical economists from Locke and adapted by Ricardo who argued, with qualifications, that the value of a commodity depended on the relative quantity of labour necessary for its production. Marx called the part of the value created which went to the employer "surplus value" and presented it as theft from the worker. The commentators do not exactly agree on the significance of the labour theory of value as it is used by Marx, but it played a key role in his predictions of capitalist self-destruction.
>
> Profits, according to the theory, are derived from unpaid labour time, yet since capitalists are driven by competition to accumulate capital and thus become more efficient in production, capital becomes concentrated in fewer and fewer hands. As it does so, the profits of capital are reduced as labour saving machinery replaces the labour from whose unpaid time profits are derived; hence, the army of the unemployed grows, swollen by the ruined small capitalist and the workers displaced by machines. The flood of goods created by ever more productive capitalist industry meanwhile find fewer buyers as more and more are workless, and wages are squeezed. United in their anger and misery, the masses rise up in revolt: "the knell of capitalist private property sounds, the expropriators are expropriated." (pp. 273-274)

This helps explain the deep Communist anger—still evident today in anti-capitalist demonstrations here and abroad—emanating from Marxist labor theory as it is based on the perceived thievery of a particularly insidious nature, that of the rich and powerful stealing from the poor and weak.

In this book, we will focus—as we always have—on the internal development of professional criminals moving toward reformation, whether consciously or unconsciously, with a specific focus on the influence Communism (in its hard and soft forms) has had on religion—especially prison ministry—the academy, and criminal justice professionals, and by extension, many criminals; all in relation to Fatima where our Holy Mother warned us about Russia, asking it to be consecrated to her Immaculate Heart , for she saw what was developing from Russia Communism without divine intervention called for through the joint prayers of Peter and all the bishops in concert.

Johnson (1991) describes Lenin as he came to Russia to take power:

> The end of the old order, with an unguided world adrift in a relativistic universe, was a summons to such gangster-statesmen to emerge. They were not slow to make their appearance...
>
> Lenin left Zurich to return to Russia on 8 April 1917...
>
> Men who carry through political revolutions seem to be of two main types, the clerical and the romantic. Lenin (he adopted the pen name in 1901) was from the first category. Both his parents were Christians. Religion was important to him, in the sense that he hated it. Unlike Marx, who despised it and treated it as marginal, Lenin saw it as a powerful and ubiquitous enemy...

> The men he really feared and hated, and later persecuted, were the saints. The purer the religion, the more dangerous. (pp.48-51)

Lenin returned to Russia April 8, 1917 and the first appearance of Our Lady of Fatima was May 13, 1917.

Our Lady saw that what was emanating from Russia was satanically powerful, and the influential power of Communism—though known by many other names, virtually a legion of names—is still alive in the prisons, woven into the doctrinal narrative of some prison gangs.

An unusual cultural aspect of criminal/carceral world culture is the power and influence the elder exerts—almost tribal like in its potency—due to the simple fact that no criminal/prisoner, hardly, ever retires due to age.

I have seen men well into their seventies and eighties (like many private corporate leaders today) who retain the physicality and intellectual heft of men decades younger.

Prison, like corporate success at the highest level, often preserves body and mind.

In the maximum security prisons, the ruling narrative of the criminal/carceral world is still exemplified and maintained by these elders, many of whom still possess the physical and mental wherewithal and most of all, the historical and cultural networks, required to exert leadership.

For many of these elders, their intellectual formation was birthed in the 1960s and the writings that emanated from that period, many of whom were written by or influenced by Communist and Communist-inspired intellectuals who saw the world in terms of class struggle and violence.

A major Communist voice during this time—and several decades prior—was Jean-Paul Sartre, about whom Kaufmann (1975) wrote:

> Finally, the greatest event in the history of existentialism since the original edition of this book appeared was *Sartre's* embrace of Marxism. (p. 9)

For decades Sartre's voice inspired the revolutionary soul of many criminals, as in his famous preface—describing the souls of the colonized who become revolutionaries—to the seminal book by Fanon (1966):

> *...this new man begins his life as a man at the end of it; he considers himself as a potential corpse. He will be killed; not only does he accept this risk, he's sure of it. This potential dead man has lost his wife and his children; he has seen so many dying men that he prefers victory to survival; others, not he, will have the fruits of victory; he is too weary of it all. But this weariness of the heart is the root of an unbelievable courage. We find our humanity on this side of death and despair; he finds it beyond torture and death. We have sown the wind; he is the whirlwind. The child of violence, at every moment he draws from it his humanity. We were men at his expense, he makes himself man at ours: a different man; of higher quality.* (Italicized in original p. 20)

I have heard variations of this central theme voiced by many professional criminals—and strongly alive within the deepest cells of super-max—as the art of being a successful criminal, a romantic fatalism in which violence is a necessary tool.

Perhaps the most important existential work read by American prisoners is *Man's Search for Meaning*, which I wrote about in a previous book, Lukenbill (2012):

The ideas have to be strong, presented with potency and clarity to even capture the attention of the criminal, and most often, initially based on a great injustice in the world that animates some of the sense of personal injustice, however unjustifiably felt, clouding the criminal's thinking.

Just such a book is *Man's Search for Meaning: An Introduction to Logotherapy,* by Viktor E. Frankl (1959).

The original title of this book was *From Death-Camp to Existentialism,* and recounted the experiences of Dr. Frankl while imprisoned in the concentration camps at Auschwitz and Dachau established by the Nazi's during the reign of Adolf Hitler.

It is a powerful book, which continues to reach out to those finding themselves in the most horrible of circumstances, with its resonating message of the fierce will to retain one's humanity, even in the most barbaric and inhuman conditions.

Studying existentialism in prison is congruent with the prison culture and it serves the purpose of beginning to study books to facilitate studying one's self.

Frankl's book is a work of existentialism, described in the Preface by Gordon W. Allport:

> It is here that we encounter the central theme of existentialism: to live is to suffer, to survive is to find meaning in the suffering. If there is a purpose in life at all, there must be a purpose in suffering and in dying. But no man can tell another what this purpose is. Each must find out for himself,

and must accept the responsibility that his answer prescribes. (p. xi)

In the concentration camps, and in a maximum security prison, this message resonates with incredible depth and clarity of meaning, and if first encountered within the deepest cell in the dark prison—the great cell of solitude in the supermax facility where I first read it—it will resonate even the more deeply.

But even here, choices can still be made, to continue with brutality and the entirely predictable response to it which always punishes the brutal, either spiritually or temporally; or to choose human kindness and allow the better angels of our nature to appear in our dealings with others and perhaps find the peace so often accompanying their exhibition.

Frankl notes:

> We who lived in concentration camps can remember the men who walked through the huts comforting others, giving away their last piece of bread. They may have been few in number, but they offer sufficient proof that everything can be taken from a man but one thing: the last of the human freedoms—to choose one's attitude in any given set of circumstances, to choose one's own way. (*Ibid.* p. 65) (Lukenbill, pp. 39-40)

No one more deeply connects existentialism to Communism and to criminals/prisoners than Sartre, most effectively in one of his magisterial works, also very popular in prison: *St. Genet: Actor and Martyr*—one of the finest studies of a certain type of criminal, which a group of us studied while I was imprisoned in McNeil Island Federal Penitentiary in the 1960s—a deeply analytical study of the criminal/artist Jean Genet, who, as noted in the end piece of the book (1963):

> This then is the man, the work, the morality, which Sartre's *Saint Genet* has undertaken to justify. Originally planned as an "introduction" to the first trade edition of Genet's novels in French, the text grew and ramified until it became Sartre's own book—in many ways his most personal and inspired, and certainly, for the non-professional reader, the most comprehensive exposition he has written of the philosophy of existentialism.
>
> For among other things, Sartre finds in Genet's life and conduct the perfect instance of the Existential Man—the human creature who consciously chooses his own selfhood and then enacts the consequences of his choice. It is in this sense that the book's subtitle calls Genet an "actor," and it is insofar as his role has been misunderstood that he is called a "martyr."

It helps explain how criminals can reach a psychological place where—except within the manipulative visions they tell for one reason or another—nothing can destroy them, certainly not prison.

One of the great classics about the path of converts to Communism who then woke up is *The God That Failed,* and one of the essays in it, Koestler (2001), notes Communism's connection to faith:

> From the psychologist's point of view, there is little difference between a revolutionary and a traditionalist faith. All true faith is uncompromising, radical, purist; hence the true traditionalist is always a revolutionary zealot in conflict with pharisaian society, with the lukewarm corrupters of the creed. And vice versa: the revolutionary's Utopia, which in appearance

represents a complete break with the past, is always modeled on some image of the lost Paradise, of a legendary Golden Age. The classless Communist society, according to Marx and Engels, was to be a revival, at the end of the dialectical spiral, of the primitive Communist society which stood at its beginning. Thus all true faith involves a revolt against the believer's social environment, and the projection into the future of an ideal derived from the remote past. All Utopias are fed from the sources of mythology; the social engineer's blueprints are merely revised editions of the ancient text. (p. 16)

From a Catholic perspective, Communism is examined as anti-faith, by Archbishop Sheen (1948):

The basic struggle today is not between individualism and collectivism, free enterprise and socialism, democracy and dictatorship. These are only the superficial manifestations of a deeper struggle which is moral and spiritual and involves above all else whether man shall exist for the state, or the state for man, and whether freedom is of the spirit or a concession of a materialized society. It has not been given to every age in history to see the issue as clearly as it has been given to our own, for we have a double incentive to work for the peace and prosperity of the world: the first is the Gospel in its fullness, the second is the communism of Soviet Russia. The first teaches us that happiness comes from living rightly; the second, that misery comes from acting wrongly. (p. 9)

In the minds of many in the West, Russian Communism disappeared when the U.S.S.R. did in the 1990s, but, as Satter (2012) notes, things are not always as they seem:

The fall of Communism left a gap in the psychology of Russians. A system that submerged the individual in the collective while encouraging him to identify with the overwhelming power of the state proved as capable of inspiring loyalty as Western democracy. The Soviet system denied the existence of universal morality and introduced a radical deprivation of freedom, but it appealed to instincts, in particular the desire for security and authority, that are no less deeply rooted and probably more basic than the drive of each person to realize himself as an individual....

Russia today has many of the characteristics of the Soviet Union, with a permanent leadership and a president for life (Putin). The socialist economy is gone, but the conception of the individual as raw material and the conviction that nothing is higher than the goals of the state continues to prevail. This made it inevitable that the moral lessons of the Soviet experience would not be learned and that Soviet habits would continue to influence the Russian population. (pp. 109 & 11)

Communism, as a way of developing power and shaping history, remains among the most insidious of Soviet habits.

Communism is the ruling mantra that China—under Stalin's tutelage—the most populous nation on earth; wakes up to each morning after being whipped and beaten into accepting it in 1949, thirty-two years after Russia brought her people under its evil yoke in 1917, the year of the apparition of our Holy Mother at Fatima.

Russia's continued involvement in Communist strategy—though it may now be more properly termed, criminal strategy—is underscored by the recent exposure of one of their spies in the United States, as noted by Wikipedia (2013).

> Anna Vasil'yevna Chapman (23 February 1982) is a Russian national who was residing in New York

City when she was arrested, along with nine others, on 27 June 2010 on suspicion of working for the Illegals Program spy ring under the Russian Federation's external intelligence agency, the SVR (Sluzhba Vneshney Razvedki). Chapman pleaded guilty to a charge of conspiracy to act as an agent of a foreign government without notifying the U.S. Attorney General, and was deported back to Russia on 8 July 2010, as part of a prisoner swap.

Chapman was born Anna Vasil'yevna Kushchyenko in Volgograd, according to U.S. authorities, and her father was employed in the Soviet embassy in Nairobi, Kenya. According to Chapman's British ex-husband, her father, Vasily Kushchenko, was a senior KGB official, although this is unsubstantiated. According to her husband, Anna Chapman Kushchyenko earned a Masters degree in economics with first class honours from Moscow University. According to other sources she got her degree from Peoples' Friendship University of Russia...

In 2012, it was reported that Chapman had almost caught a senior member of President Obama's cabinet in a honeytrap operation. The plan would have involved Chapman seducing her target before extracting information from him. However, it was foiled before execution (n.p.)

Retrieved May 27, 2013 from http://en.wikipedia.org/wiki/Anna_Chapman

The strategies developed and released into the world through the Communist International—known as the Comintern—over the many decades that dramatically shaped Russia under Lenin and Stalin, are strategies that continue; though the dividends may not be classified as revolutionary, as under the International, they are effective economically, politically and powerfully influential.

One of Catholicism's most perceptive American thinkers, John Courtney Murray, S. J. (1960) wrote:

> It would be impossible to set limits to the danger of Communism as a spiritual menace. It has induced not simply a crisis in history but perhaps the crisis of history. Its dream of the Third Epoch that will cancel Western and Christian history and the major institutions of that history (Notably the rule of law and the spiritual supremacy of the Church) has gone too far toward realization over too wide a sweep of earth to be lightly dismissed as a mere dream. (p. 244)

And today, in 2013, fully fifty-three years since those words were published, Communism and its Socialistic method of government, its Marxist method of historical criticism, its violent form of revolution when called for—as today in the third world—its state control of religion, and its deep atheism, is still a very powerful enemy of the Church.

It is not just that it is a godless ideology, but that it is—since its introduction into the world—the most influential advocate of materialistic atheism intent on destroying the Catholic Church; and whatever name Communism works under, and they are legion, it seeks a final solution.

Though, as Reagan described it, the evil empire (the U.S.S.R.) was broken up under the leadership of Pope John Paul II, President Ronald Reagan, and Prime Minister Margaret Thatcher, the evil idea underlying it—total government control, including over religion—remains active in the world, exercising direct control over more than one billion people and indirectly hundreds of millions more.

One of its most potent weapons being used today, emanating from its Stalinist past, is the practice of disinformation, which produces incorrect information to cast aspersions on the enemies of Communism, primarily the Catholic Church and America.

An excellent example was the black church burnings of the 1990s, outlined by Pacepa & Rychlak (2013):

> In March 1996, a sensational story jolted the American conscience. The National Council of Churches (NCC) and the Center for Democratic Renewal (CDR), two secretly Marxist organizations headquartered in the United States held a joint press conference to announce a "huge increase" in the number of arson cases committed against black churches in the United States....
>
> The story spread like wildfire...
>
> On July 13, President Clinton signed into law the Church Fire Prevention Act of 1996, which made church arson a federal crime. On August 7, he also signed a spending bill that included $12 million to combat fires at churches with black congregations. A few days later the NCC ran full-page ads in the *New York Times, Washington Post* and numerous other papers soliciting donations for its new "Burned Churches Fund." On August 9, the *Wall Street Journal* reported that the NCC had "managed to raise nearly $9 million," and that contributions were continuing to pour in "at about $100,000 a day."
>
> Then the bubble burst. It was eventually established by a private group, the National Fire Protection Association, that in recent years there had been far *fewer* church fires than usual, and law enforcement officials in the South could not confirm *any* as having been racially motivated. No Church burning had occurred in Arkansas during Clinton's childhood, in spite of his "vivid and painful" memories, and the National Council of

> Churches was accused of fabricating a "great church-fire hoax."...
>
> The clue to understanding the significance of the black church arson hoax lies in the documented fact that the World Council of Churches, which ignited and promoted that story, has been infiltrated and ultimately controlled by Russian intelligence since 1961...In fact, in 1972 Soviet intelligence managed to have Metropolitan Nikodim (its agent "Adamant") elected WCC president. (pp. 1-3)

Russian disinformation was also at the root of the largely successful campaign, until recently, convincing many that Pope Pius XII was an anti-Semite when he personally saved many Jewish lives and worked vigorously against Nazism.

Communism has used it effectively.

> Since World War II, *disinformation* has been the Kremlin's most effective weapon in its war on the West, especially on Western religion. Iosif Stalin invented this secret "science," giving it a French-sounding name and pretending it was a dirty Western practice...the Kremlin has secretly, and successfully, calumniated leading Roman Catholic prelates, culminating in Pope Pius XII; it almost succeeded in assassinating Pope John Paul II; it invented liberation theology, a Marxist doctrine that turned many European and Latin American Catholics against the Vatican and the United States; it has promoted anti-Semitism and international terrorism; and it has inspired anti-American uprisings in the Islamic world. (*Ibid.* p. 5)

This idea of the essential evil of Catholic leadership and American leadership also retains influence within the cultural heights of American—and even more deeply in European and Asian—public life, in the academy, government, media, religion, and to a surprising depth within Catholicism itself.

The primary tools used in the political propaganda wars that pit right against left and the Catholic Church against atheists and secular governments—where demonization is the normative argument of left against right in the Catholic Church in America—are tools developed most effectively in the last century by Communism.

In this book, we are specifically focusing on Russian Communism, as that is what the Holy Mother of God warned us about at Fatima, and that is the Communism that is the intellectual father of all of the others, deeply engaged since its founding on spreading its revolution worldwide; a revolution that has led, in Russia itself, to the criminal corruption endemic to atheistic governments, as Satter (2003) writes:

> Gangsters in Russia are not a marginal phenomenon confined to such area of the illegal economy as narcotics, prostitution, and gun running. They control large parts of the legitimate economy, and neither a powerless public nor the organs of law enforcement have the means to bring them under control.
>
> In 1997, 9,000 criminal groups in Russia with nearly 600,000 members controlled an estimated 40 percent of the Russian economy. The U.S. Central Intelligence Agency estimated that more than half of Russia's twenty-five largest banks were either directly tied to organized crime or engaged in other illegal activity. (p. 131)

The Church has gone from a clear denunciation of Russian Communism by Peter during the 19th and the early 20th century to an accommodation with it immediately prior to and since Vatican II.

The language the Church uses today is congruent with that used in the Garden where God spoke clearly, but where Satan, using flattery, deception, and persuasion, seduced Adam and Eve to disregard that clarity and seek the hidden meaning behind the Word.

To more effectively combat Satan for souls, the Church has learned to use the arts of persuasion.

History will tell if this is a wise change of direction by the Church and it may very well be; but because of the failure to follow the warnings of the Holy Mother at Fatima of what would happen if the Holy Father and all the bishops did not consecrate Russia to her Immaculate Heart, warnings which history has shown to be true, we have to wonder what future history will reveal.

It has been my experience, through personal interaction with many Catholics, and academic study, that Communist-inspired Liberation Theology, working through the social justice mantra as developed by Communist-inspired Catholics in America, Asia, and Europe, and further elaborated by many religious throughout the Church, with particular depth in Latin America, that Communism is alive and well within the Church.

Professional criminals catechized with this form of Catholicism—with its restorative justice, prison and capital punishment abolition, and social causation rather than individual choice, approach to crime—which, though they may respond to initially, does not possess the clarity, depth, or truth, that will hold for the long term.

The reason for that is connected to the focus of this apostolate on the professional criminal, excluding pedophiles, rapists, and informers; for professional criminals who have served time in maximum security prisons, whose abhorrence for sexual predators and those who betray their brothers in crime, extends to the death, would not become part of an apostolate who welcomed those who they so strongly reject.

The Lampstand Foundation's work focuses on professional criminals who commit crimes for money as professional criminals constitute the majority of criminals (approximately 70%) housed in state and federal prisons, and professional criminals have the credibility, in prison or out, to authentically communicate with other criminals about personal reformation and conversion through the Catholic Church, or as we like to say, "It takes a reformed criminal to reform criminals."

According to the latest statistics from the U.S. Department of Justice, (Carson & Sabol, December 2012) there were 1,537,415 criminals incarcerated in state and federal prisons as of December 31, 2011.

1,095,600 (71.26 %) of them were incarcerated for crimes where the acquisition of money is the primary motivation—including murder/assault (we estimate that 50% of murders and assaults are committed for the underlying reason of gaining, expanding, or protecting criminal turf or proceeds) robbery, property crimes, drug crimes (most of which, including possession, involve possession with intent to sell) weapons charges, and public order charges (which include prostitution and pandering).

Much of the lure of Communism to the poor and oppressed people of the world is their yearning for freedom and peace in this world—a yearning exploited by many prison ministries—and though the Communist government that so often assumes control of a country's revolution, becomes as great a tyrant as the oppressor they revolted against; this yearning for peace and freedom is deeply real and not to be discounted.

I recently finished a book by West (2013) which lays the cause of the successful penetration of Communism into American government and society at the feet of the presidential administration of Franklin Delano Roosevelt because FDR was captivated by 'Uncle Joe' Stalin and many of FDR's top advisors were Communists themselves and her very well researched case is a strong one; but even with the presidential aid, scarcely a few decades later Russia Communism morphed into open gangsterism—its essential and long hidden heart; and the looming threat of a Communist Russia annihilating Western civilization seems to be well over as the intent of criminals is merely to be allowed to manage and expand their criminal turf with little interference.

Feeding the beast satiates him and though he gets hungry again, it is as much from habit, than from the old 'lean and hungry look' that motivated him to feed again.

As God allows Satan to prey on us, earthly empires often allow enemies to prey on the weak and this is where the promise of justice in eternity rings as true, for the rewards for Satan of evil souls to extend his turf are also rewards for God as saints arise from the ancient war between good and evil.

Yet, West (2013) reminds us of the need for eternal vigilance:

> In the following quotation, Robert Conquest, circa 2005, is retrospectively considering the animus of Soviet Communism, but what he describes sounds much like the timeless drive of Islamic jihad:
>
>> The confrontation with the West was, like the ruin of the [Soviet] economy, a product of the mental distortions of the Soviet order. The 'insane militarization' Gorbachev spoke of was a symptom of the mind-set that prevailed, which required *an unceasing struggle with all other cultures* [emphasis added].

> One salient difference is that the Soviets only had "rope" to sell the West; Islam has oil.
>
> While there is reasonable consensus on the link between the Soviets' "unceasing struggle" with others (climaxing in the Reagan-driven arms race) and the ultimate ruin of the Soviet economy, we hardly consider the impact that this same "unceasing struggle" had on ourselves. The fact is, wars change combatants, and we, the West, did not emerge unscathed from the better part of a century of accommodating, appeasing, enabling, opposing, fighting, tolerating, accepting, and assisting the influence and power of the Soviet regime. Indeed, the changes wrought by this continuous entanglement of Communist Russia and the Free World are deep, if also grossly and dangerously underappreciated.
>
> Take the reputation in the West of Communism itself. It may not be trumpeted as the coming thing—not specifically by name anyway—but, in the burn pit for catastrophic ideologies, its aura today is not blackened to the same crisp as Nazism and fascism. Not even close. Despite Soviet "defeat" in 1991, the ideas associated with Communism remain shockingly reputable throughout what we still know as the Free World. (p. 21)

And quoting a 2010 speech by the Netherland's Geert Wilders, West writes:

> Islam is the Communism of today. But because of our failure to come clean with Communism, we are unable to deal with it, trapped as we are in the old Communist habit of deceit and double-speak that used to haunt the countries in the East and that now haunts all of us. (*Ibid.* p. 346)

Professional criminals, especially those at the higher levels of the criminal corporate structure, understand the immoral global power politics utilized by Communism, and will be drawn to a truth that can compete globally, as McGregor (2010) notes:

> It is no coincidence that the Vatican is one of the few states with which China has been unable to establish diplomatic ties since the founding of the People's Republic in 1949. The city-state, which is the administrative centre of the Catholic Church and the home of the Pope, is the only other organization of comparable dimensions to the Chinese Communist Party, albeit on a global scale, and with a similar addiction to ritual and secrecy. The party guards the command of its catechism as zealously and self-righteously as the Vatican defends its authority over the faith. After years of on-and-off talks, the Vatican has not been able to reconcile its worldwide prerogative to appoint bishops with the Party's insistence that it alone has the right to approve their choice for the Catholic Church at home in China. The on-and-off-again talks between Rome and Beijing have been punctuated, in private, by a self-aware black humour. One of the unofficial Chinese intermediaries with Rome joked about the uncanny similarities between the Party and the Catholic Church when he visited the Vatican in 2008. 'We have the propaganda department and you have the evangelicals. We have the organization [personnel] department and you have the College of Cardinals,' he told a Vatican official. 'What's the difference, then?' the official asked. The Chinese interlocutor replied, to hearty laughter all round: 'You are God, and we are the devil!' (p. 11)

Solzhenitsyn (1976) speaking to American audiences in 1975 and 1976, warned them about what he knew, from his searing personal experience, about the Russian Communists:

> Communism has never concealed the fact that it rejects all absolute concepts of morality. It scoffs at any consideration of "good" and "evil" as indisputable categories. Communism considers morality to be relative, to be a class matter. Depending upon circumstances and the political situation, any act, including murder, even the killing of hundreds of thousands, could be good or could be bad. It all depends upon class ideology. And who defines this ideology? The whole class cannot get together to pass judgment. A handful of people determine what is good and what is bad. But I must say that in this very respect Communism has been most successful. It has infected the whole world with the belief in the relativity of good and evil. Today, many people apart from the Communists are carried away by this idea. Among progressive people, it is considered rather awkward to use seriously such words as "good" and "evil". Communism has managed to persuade all of us that these concepts are old-fashioned and laughable. But if we are deprived of the concepts of good and evil, what will be left? Nothing but the manipulation of each other. We will sink to the status of animals. (pp. 57-58)

Russia also reads the words of its severest critics and, in the spirit of accommodation and with its reliable tools of deception and misdirection, continues in fine form, as Kishkovsky (2013) notes, writing about Russia's President Putin speaking at an event in July of 2013 celebrating Christianity in Russia:

> He described Communism "as just a simplified version of the religious principles shared by practically all the world's traditional religions" and said that today's turn to religion was "a

> spontaneous movement from the people themselves to turn back to their roots" in response to the ideological vacuum after the Soviet Union's collapse in 1991. (p. A-4)

Finally, the contemporary influence of Communism among some of the most organized of former criminals is revealed through the Marxian analysis describing how criminals are constructed socially, from Murphy, Richards, & Fuleihan (2012):

> American society typically relegates criminals to the bottom of the political and social power structure where they are typically considered ineligible or deemed the least deserving of most social benefits...and receive a disproportionate share of burdens and sanctions. The widespread growth of criminal history repositories and their low-cost access have further eroded possible opportunities or avenues for persons convicted of crimes for personal and social empowerment, even when they have changed their ways. Criminals are labeled as incorrigible deviants. The public would like to think that they are a separate species, persons unlike themselves, different and damaged. (p. 90)

In Marxian analysis individuals at the bottom of the social ladder—and in America, it is most surely and most thankfully, still a ladder—are helpless players in the movement of social forces controlled by the rich capitalists and the officialdom they control; while the reality is that crime is a result of individual choice, and rehabilitation, true transformation from being a member of the criminal/carceral world to joining the communal world, is always solely within the power of the individual, as it has always been, as it always will be.

Communism in Russia

Russia and the Communist system of governance which Our Lady warned us about at Fatima while calling for Russia to be consecrated to her Immaculate Heart, evolved within a history of autocracy that began, as Szamuely (1974) writes:

> The synthesis of the Muscovite seigneurial system, of Mongol despotism and of Byzantine Caesaropapism, in the distinctive form of Russian autocracy, can be said to have first emerged, after a lengthy period of germination, in the middle of the sixteenth century. More than any other man, it owes its crystallization, both in theory and in practice, to Ivan the Terrible. Whatever posterity may have had to say about Ivan—and its judgment has tended, with every reason, to be a harsh one—there can be no denying the fact that he was a great innovator, even a great revolutionary in the field of government. Ivan left an imprint on Russia that 400 years have failed to erase.
>
> Ivan, a man of considerable education, expounded his views on autocracy, at great length, in one of the most remarkable political documents of Russian history: his correspondence with Prince Kurbsky, a former favourite, who had fled to Lithuania to escape the Tsar's wrath (thus becoming probably the first Russian political defector). From the safety of the West Kurbsky bitterly attacked the Tsar in print, accusing him of having renounced Russia's ancient political traditions, of ruling arbitrarily, without seeking the advice of the boyars, of reducing all to the level of slaves, etc. Stung to the quick, Ivan replied in even more abusive terms. Very cleverly, but in complete contradiction of the facts, he set out to prove that he was only following

in the footsteps of his ancestors, each of whom, since time immemorial, had possessed absolute, unlimited power; he also gave an entirely new interpretation of the title of autocrat: previously it had only meant a sovereign ruler in his own right, independent of any suzerain—now, for the first time , Ivan took it to mean an absolute despotic ruler, governing his country as he saw fit, with no bounds set to his authority over his subjects, their lives and their property. Indeed, he made it eminently clear that his subjects, however high their station, were no better than slaves, and their property—his to take at any time he deemed fit...

In a country without any basic constitutional laws, where for centuries no attempt was made to define the political system, the structure and functions of government, or even the relationship between government and subjects, the writings of Ivan the Terrible remained until comparatively recent times the most forthright and authoritative exposition of the all-embracing powers of the Russian State, embodied in the person of the autocratic monarch. It was a new and revolutionary concept of government, which, although already partially realized in practice, was undoubtedly foreign to the political system that had existed in Ancient Rus. Needless to say, Ivan's doctrine of the State as legitimate proprietor of all that lay or moved within its territories had hardly anything in common with Western theories of the divine right of kings, theories that derived from an entirely different system of social relationships. (pp. 30-31)

Szamuely opens his book with an extensive quote from one of the great books on Russia in the 19th Century, *Empire of the Czar: A Journey Through Eternal Russia*, written by the Marquis de Custine in 1839, after his travels through Russia:

The political state of Russia may be defined in one sentence: it is a country in which the government says what it pleases, because it alone has the right to speak...

In Russia, power, all unlimited as it is, entertains an extreme dread of censure, or even of free speech...I compare, with a wonder mixed with fear, the disorder of ideas that reigns among us, with the absence of all private views, of all personal opinion—the blind submission, in short, which forms the rule of conduct among all, whether heads or subordinates, who carry on the administration of affairs in Russia...

In Russia, fear replaces, that is, paralyses thought...

Here reserve is the order of the day, just as imprudence is in Paris. In Russia secrecy presides over everything; a silence that is superfluous insures the silence that is necessary...

The corps diplomatique, and the Western people in general, have always been considered by this Byzantine government and by Russia in general, as malignant and jealous spies...

In Russia, on the day that a minister falls from favour, his friends become deaf and blind. No one dares to remember that he is living, nor even to believe that he ever had lived. A man is as it were buried the moment he appears to be disgraced. Russia does not know today if the minister who governed her yesterday exists...

Nor in this country is historical truth any better respected than the sanctity of oaths...even the dead are exposed to the fantasies of him who rules the living...

> When the sun of publicity shall rise upon Russia, how many injustices will it expose to view!—not only ancient ones, but those which are enacted daily will shock the senses of the world. (*Ibid.* pp. 3-4)

Though this was written in 1839, virtually all of it was true of the Russian Empire under Communism and one fears, it is still true today.

One of the most perceptive of writers on Russian Communism was the Russian religious and political philosopher Nicolas Berdyaev (1960), who wrote:

> Russian Communism is difficult to understand on account of its twofold nature. On the one hand it is international and a world phenomenon; on the other hand it is national and Russian. It is particularly important for Western minds to understand the national roots of Russian Communism and the fact that it was Russian history which determined its limits and shaped its character. A knowledge of Marxism will not help in this. The Russian people in their spiritual make-up are an Eastern people. Russia is the Christian East, which was for two centuries subject to the powerful influences of the West, and whose cultured classes assimilated every Western idea. The fate of the Russian people in history has been an unhappy one and full of suffering. It has developed at a catastrophic tempo through interruption and change in its type of civilization. (p. 7)

Russian Communism has had particular success reshaping the worldly ground upon which the Church stands, as Joseph Cardinal Ratzinger (1996) wrote:

> After the Second World War, humanity was divided ever more sharply into two camps; into a world of affluent peoples, who for the most part were once more living according to the liberal model, and into

the Marxist block, which conceived of itself both as the spokesman of the poor nations of South America, Africa and Asia and as their model for the future. Correspondingly, there arose a twofold division of theological tendencies.

In the neoliberal world of the West, a variant of the former liberal theology now became operative in a new guise: the eschatological interpretation of Jesus' message. Jesus, it is true, is no longer conceived as a pure moralist, yet he is once again construed in opposition to the cult and the historical institutions of the Old Testament. This interpretation was a revamping of the old framework that breaks up the Old Testament into priests and prophets: into cult, institution and law, on the one hand, and prophecy, charism and creative freedom, on the other. In this view, priests, cult and institution appear as the negative factor that must be overcome. Jesus, on the other hand, supposedly stands in the prophetic line and fulfills it in antithesis to the priesthood, which is said to have done away with him as it had the prophets.

A new variety of individualism thus comes into being: Jesus now proclaims the end of the institutions. Though his eschatological message may have been conceived according to the end of the world, it is retrieved for our day as the revolutionary breakthrough from the institutional realm into the charismatic dimension, as the end of the religions, or, in any case, as "unworldly faith" that is ceaselessly re-creating its own forms. Once again there can be no question of the foundation of a Church; such an act would, in fact, contradict this eschatological radicalness.

But this new version of liberalism was quite susceptible to being converted into a Marxist-oriented interpretation of the bible. The opposition

> between priests and prophets became a cipher for the class struggle, which is taken to be the law of history. Accordingly, Jesus lost his life engaged in combat against the forces of oppression. He is thus transformed into the symbol of the suffering and struggling proletariat, of the "people", as is now more commonly said. The eschatological character of the message then refers to the end of the class-society; the prophet-priest dialectic expresses the dialectic of history, which comes to its final conclusion with the victory of the oppressed and with the emergence of the classless society. The fact that Jesus hardly mentioned the Church, but spoke repeatedly of the Kingdom of God, can be very easily integrated into this view: the "Kingdom" is the classless society, which is held out as the objective toward which the downtrodden people struggles; it is considered as already existing wherever the organized proletariat, that is, its party, socialism, has triumphed.
>
> Ecclesiology now becomes newly significant: it is fitted into the dialectical framework already set up by the division of the Bible into priests and prophets, which is then conflated with a corresponding distinction between institution and people. In accordance with this dialectical model, the "popular Church", this "popular Church" is ceaselessly born out of the people and in this way carried forward Jesus' cause: his struggle against institutions and their oppressive power for the sake of a new and free society that will be the "Kingdom". (pp. 16-19)

This vision of Jesus as revolutionary embroiled in a Marxist struggle to free the people from the powers of the rich and powerful, including the priests of Israel and the Roman Empire, is a powerful motif and attracts many to its ranks, a message continuing today to be promulgated through books, film, and theatre.

The continuing influence emanating from the atheistic intellectual and artistic community is part of the reason Our Lady of Fatima told us to consecrate Russia, as Russian Communism is the most dangerous manifestation of the ancient heresy, primarily intellectually elite in nature, of Gnosticism, described by Arendzen (1909):

> Whereas Judaism and Christianity, and almost all pagan systems, hold that the soul attains its proper end by obedience of mind and will to the Supreme Power, i.e. by faith and works, it is markedly peculiar to Gnosticism that it places the salvation of the soul merely in the possession of a quasi-intuitive knowledge of the mysteries of the universe and of magic formulae indicative of that knowledge. Gnostics were "people who knew", and their knowledge at once constituted them a superior class of beings, whose present and future status was essentially different from that of those who, for whatever reason, did not know. (n.p.)

Communism's religiosity, its modern spiritual root, birthed from Gnosticism, but woven throughout another influence, is Nietzschean, the atheistic, materialist spirituality of the Overman, the man who knows, as Nietzsche (1959) writes:

> When Zarathustra came into the next town, which lies on the edge of the forest, he found many people gathered together in the market place; for it had been promised that there would be a tightrope walker. And Zarathustra spoke thus to the people:
>
> "*I teach you the overman.* Man is something that shall be overcome. What have you done to overcome him?
>
> "All beings so far have created something beyond themselves; and do you want to be the ebb of this great flood and even go back to the beasts rather than overcome man? What is the ape to man? A

> laughingstock or a painful embarrassment. And man shall be just that for the overman: a laughingstock or a painful embarrassment. You have made your way from worm to man, and much in you is still worm. Once you were apes, and even now, too, man is more ape than any ape.
>
> "Whoever is the wisest among you is also a mere conflict and cross between plant and ghost. But do I bid you become ghost or plant?
>
> "Behold, I teach you the overman. The overman is the meaning of the earth. Let your will say: the overman *shall be* the meaning of the earth! I beseech you, my brothers, *remain faithful to the earth*, and do not believe those who speak to you of otherworldly hopes! Poison-mixers are they, whether they know it or not. Despisers of life are they, decaying and poisoned themselves, of whom the earth is weary: so let them go.
>
> "Once the sin against God was the greatest sin; but God died, and these sinners died with him. To sin against the earth is now the most dreadful thing, and to esteem the entrails of the unknowable higher than the meaning of the earth. (pp. 124-125)

A historical infection endemic to the Russian Communist state—as of all Communist states—in congruence with its militant atheistic core beliefs, is corruption and criminality, and Russia has morphed into the most potent criminal state in history, dominating the global criminal world, as Sterling (1994) writes:

> Liberated Russia, as the underworld's new country of choice, is becoming an active danger to its Western friends. There is no way for Western law enforcement agencies to investigate, still less pursue, their own criminals drifting east. They have no lawful right to do it and until very recently did

> not much care. Their Eastern counterparts have practically no suitable laws of their own, no money, pitiful equipment, and hardly any properly trained personnel. There are no provisions for extradition on either side, and next to none for exchanging police and intelligence information.
>
> In effect, then, the big syndicates have come upon a safe house the size of Western Europe and America combined where they can dodge the cops, meet, plan strategy, work out new drug routes, manage their money, settle territorial disputes, and carve up the planet undisturbed, all of which they appear to be doing.
>
> The shift has come so swiftly that Western investigators can hardly take it in. Because the Sicilian Mafia still towers over the underworld, many still believe that the center of worldwide criminal power is Italy. In the autumn of 1993, however, the head of Italy's Parliamentary Anti-Mafia Commission made it plain that the venue had changed. "The world capital of organized crime is Russia," he said. (p. 17)

This shift has ramifications of enormous consequence, and the role of the Catholic Church, because of the knowledge bequeathed to it by Our Lady at Fatima, is crucial.

Fatima is a miracle believed by faith, but investigating it with the intellect reveals proofs of its existence impossible to escape; just as an intellectual exploration of Communism reveals an evil emptiness impossible to escape.

As the primary process of reformation used by Lampstand is through the intellectual portal to the soul, based on a study of the history and social teaching of the Church, graduate academic degrees, and training in criminal reform organizational administration; the intellectual attraction of Communism and its many portals—socialism, Marxism, and Liberation Theology among them—needs to be addressed.

Storck (2013) notes the importance of the intellect in approaching Catholic truth from the perspective of the father of Western intellectuals, Aristotle, and the seminal Catholic intellectual, Saint Thomas Aquinas, the Angelic Doctor:

> In Aristotle and Thomas's understanding of man, our faculty of choosing, is subordinate to the intellect, and chooses that real or apparent good that the intellect presents to it. This is a seemingly arcane proposition, but it is in fact one of the highest importance. For if the will were the primary element in our choice of good and evil, then morality would, at its most basic level, be irrational, not a matter of knowledge but of choice, and thus ultimately of power and caprice. But by asserting the primacy of the intellect in choosing good and thereby instructing the will as to the choice it should make, Aristotle and Thomas were safeguarding man's essential rationality by refusing to abandon morality either to the will, to power, or to blind adherence to a textual command recorded in Scripture, as evangelical protestants largely do. (p. 25)

Further defining the ground, here are definitions from Brown (1993):

> **Communism:** (A theory advocating) a system of society with property vested in the community and each member working for the common benefit according to his or her needs; *spec.* (usu. **C-**) the movement or political party advocating such a system, esp. as derived from Marxism and seeking the overthrow of capitalism by a proletarian revolution; the communistic form of society

established in the 20th century in the former USSR and elsewhere. (p. 455)

Liberation Theology: A theory, originating among Latin American theologians, which interprets liberation from social, political, and economic oppression as an anticipation of eschatological salvation. (*Ibid.* p. 1577)

Marxism: The political and economic theories of the German-born writer Karl Marx (1818-83), esp. that, as labour is basic to wealth, historical development must lead to the violent overthrow of the capitalist class and the taking over of the means of production by the proletariat, in accordance with scientific laws determined by dialectical materialism. (*Ibid.* p. 1705)

Socialism: A political and economic theory or policy of social organization which advocates that the community as a whole should own and control the means of production, capital, land, property, etc. Also *spec.* in Marxist theory, a transitional social state between the overthrow of capitalism and the realization of communism. (*Ibid.* p. 2931)

Wikipedia puts all of this into context in its entries on Communism and Liberation Theology:

Communism (from Latin *communis* - common, universal) is a revolutionary socialist movement to create a classless, moneyless, and stateless social order structured upon common ownership of the means of production, as well as a social, political and economic ideology that aims at the establishment of this social order. This movement, in its Marxist-Leninist interpretations, significantly influenced the history of the 20th century, which saw intense rivalry between the "socialist world" (socialist states ruled by communist parties) and the "western world" (countries with capitalist economies).

Marxist theory holds that pure communism or full communism is a specific stage of historical development that inevitably emerges from the development of the productive forces that leads to a superabundance of material wealth, allowing for distribution based on need and social relations based on freely associated individuals. The exact definition of communism varies, and it is often mistakenly, in general political discourse, used interchangeably with socialism; however, Marxist theory contends that socialism is just a transitional stage on the road to communism. Leninism adds to Marxism the notion of a vanguard party to lead the proletarian revolution and to secure all political power after the revolution for the working class, for the development of universal class consciousness and worker participation, in a transitional stage between capitalism and socialism.

Retrieved August 24, 2012 from http://en.wikipedia.org/wiki/Communism

Liberation theology is a political movement in Catholic theology which interprets the teachings of Jesus Christ in terms of a liberation from unjust economic, political, or social conditions. It has been described by proponents as "an interpretation of Christian faith through the poor's suffering, their struggle and hope, and a critique of society and the Catholic faith and Christianity through the eyes of the poor", and by detractors as Christianized Marxism.

Although liberation theology has grown into an international and inter-denominational movement, it began as a movement within the Catholic Church in Latin America in the 1950s–1960s. Liberation theology arose principally as a moral reaction to the poverty caused by social injustice in that region. The term was coined in 1971 by the Peruvian priest Gustavo Gutiérrez, who wrote one of the movement's most famous books, *A Theology of Liberation*. Other noted exponents are Leonardo Boff of Brazil, Jon Sobrino of El Salvador, Óscar Romero of El Salvador, and Juan Luis Segundo of Uruguay.

The influence of liberation theology diminished after proponents were accused of using "Marxist concepts" leading to admonishment by the Vatican's Congregation for the Doctrine of the Faith (CDF) in 1984 and 1986. The Vatican criticized certain strains of liberation theology for focusing on institutionalized or systemic sin, apparently to the exclusion of individual offenders/offences; and for allegedly misidentifying Catholic Church hierarchy in South America as members of the same privileged class that had long been oppressing indigenous populations since the arrival of Pizarro onward.

Retrieved January 19, 2013 from http://en.wikipedia.org/wiki/Liberation_theology

An interesting side note is that for a brief period of time in the 1960s/1970s, especially in California, criminals were seen as *the vanguard* of the revolution, as Cummins (1994) writes:

> Bay Area radicals were very clear about what kind of revolutionary prisoner-leader they were looking for in 1970. Ho Chi Minh's phrase had been circulating for year: "When the prison gates fly open, the real dragons will emerge." At the war's end radicals assumed that what was true for Ho's

> Vietnam also held in the United States: political captives constituted the majority of inmates, and they would be the best foot soldiers for American revolution. (p. 153)

Mises (1981) in his seminal work on Socialism, notes:

> In the terminology of Marx and Engels the words communism and socialism are synonymous. They are alternately applied without any distinction between them. The same was true for the practice of all Marxian groups and sects until 1917. The political parties of Marxism which considered the Communist Manifesto as the unalterable doctrine called themselves socialist parties. The most influential and most numerous of these parties, the German party, adopted the name Social Democratic Party. In Italy, in France and in all other countries in which Marxian parties already played a role in political life before 1917, the term socialist likewise superseded the term communist. No Marxian ever ventured, before 1917, to distinguish between communism and socialism....

> One of the fundamental dogmas of Marx is that socialism is bound to come "with the inexorability of a law of nature." (Das Kapital) Capitalist production begets its own negation and establishes the socialist system of public ownership of the means of production. This process "executes itself through the operation of the inherent laws of capitalist production." (*Ibid.*) It is independent of the wills of people. It is impossible for men to accelerate it, to delay it or to hinder it. For "no social system ever disappears before all the productive forces are developed for the development of which it is broad enough, and new higher methods of production never appear before the material conditions of their existence have been hatched out in the womb of previous society."

> This doctrine is, of course, irreconcilable with Marx's own political activities and with the teachings he advanced for the justification of these activities. Marx tried to organize a political party which by means of revolution and civil war should accomplish the transition from capitalism to socialism. The characteristic feature of their parties was, in the eyes of Marx and all Marxian doctrinaires, that they were revolutionary parties invariably committed to the idea of violent action. Their aim was to rise in rebellion, to establish the dictatorship of the proletarians and to exterminate mercilessly all bourgeois. The deeds of the Paris Communards in 1871 were considered as the perfect model of such a civil war. (pp. 497-498)

What this makes clear is that the common usage of the term Socialism or Marxism rather than Communism can be deceptive—to either soften or intellectualize the reality—so we'll use them as intended by Marx and Engels, as synonymous, while keeping in mind modern usage.

Russian Communism was identified by Our Lady of Fatima as a most pernicious threat to the Church, a position ratified by several popes, but later, during Vatican II softened and virtually disappearing as a papal warning.

Communism in America

Fr. Murray (1960) explains why Soviet doctrine had such a powerful influence, especially over potential Fifth Column movements outside of Russia:

> It has exhibited a new mastery of older imperialistic techniques—military conquest, the enduring threat of force, political puppetry, centralized administration of minorities, economic exploitation of "colonial" regions. It has expanded the old concept of "ally" into the new concept of the "satellite." But perhaps its newness is chiefly revealed in the creation of the historically unique imperialistic device known as "Soviet patriotism." This is not a thing of blood and soil but of mind and spirit. It is not born of the past, its deeds and sufferings borne in common; it looks more to the future, to the deeds yet to be done and to the sufferings still to be borne. It is a "patriotism of a higher order," and of a more universal bearing, than any of the classic feelings for *das Vaterland, la patrie,* my country. It is a loyalty to the Socialist Revolution; it is also a loyalty to the homeland of the Revolution, Russia. Its roots are many—in ideology, in economic facts, and in the love of power; in a whole cluster of human resentments and idealisms; and in the endless capacities of the human spirit for ignorance, illusion, and self-deception. This higher patriotism claims priority over all mere national loyalties. It assures to the Soviet Union a form of imperialistic penetration into other states, namely the Fifth Column, that no government in history has hitherto commanded. Soviet imperialism, unlike former imperialisms, can be content with the creation of chaos and

> disorder; within any given segment of time it need not seek to impose a dominion, an order. The Soviet Union may indeed lack a finished imperial design; in any case, the concept of design is too rational for a force that owes little to reason. But it has something better for its purposes, which are inherently dark. It has a revolutionary vision. (p. 225)

Many Catholics—especially those from the prime era of Soviet influence, the 1930s-1970s—who were caught up in the Nietzschean drama of Communism and later in its newest incarnation, Liberation Theology, liked to say that the horrors of Leninism/Stalinism were vestiges of the past and necessary to reform a tsarist dominated peoples into a modern industrialized society, but Fr. Murray clears up that misconception also:

> Moreover, it will not do to say that this dictation of policy and events by doctrine will not happen again; that Stalin is dead; that Russia is "different"; that new men are in charge; that they are realists and opportunists, men rather like ourselves who take the pragmatic view. Russia is indeed somewhat different, but only within the limits of the doctrine. The men in charge are new, but only within the limits imposed by their thorough conditioning by the doctrine. The Soviet leadership is not subject to changes of heart. What is more important (and to the pragmatist, unintelligible), it does not even learn by experience. The doctrine is forever at hand to discount Soviet experience of how the capitalist world acts.
>
> The doctrine casts up an image of the capitalist world that does not derive from experience and is not to be altered by experience. It is a "scientific" image, the product of a science, dialectical materialism, whose basic postulate is that determinism rules the world of human history as

well as the world of nature. It is through the distorting one-way glass, as it were, of this deterministic theory of capitalism that the Soviet leaders view what we consider to be the contingencies of the historical world—only they are not seen as contingencies but as determined. So far from altering the scientific image, they are interpreted in such a way as either to confirm it or at least leave it intact. When, for instance, the capitalist world professes its desire to be friendly, just, peaceful, cooperative, etc., such professions cannot but be bogus. Historical determinism will not permit the capitalist world to be other than hostile, unjust, aggressive, and war-mongering. (*Ibid.* p. 231)

Whittaker Chambers (1952) describes Communist attraction in personal terms, as he was once a deeply loyal Communist:

> [A] man does not, as a rule, become a Communist because he is attracted to Communism, but because he is driven to despair by the crisis of history through which the world is passing....
>
> In the West, all intellectuals become Communists because they are seeking the answer to one of two problems: the problem of war or the problem of economic crisis....
>
> Under pressure of the crisis, his decision to become a Communist seems to the man who makes it as a choice between a world that is dying and a world that is coming to birth, as an effort to save by political surgery whatever is sound in the foredoomed body of a civilization which nothing less drastic can save—a civilization foredoomed first of all by its reluctance to face the fact that the crisis exists or to face it with the force and clarity necessary to overcome it.

> Thus, the Communist Party presents itself as the one organization with the will to survive the crisis in a civilization where that will is elsewhere divided, wavering or absent. It is in the name of that will to survive the crisis, which is not theoretical but closes in from all sides, that the Communist first justifies the use of terror and tyranny, which are repugnant to most men by nature and which the whole tradition of the West specifically repudiates....
>
> It is the crisis that makes men Communists and it is the crisis that keeps men Communists. For the Communist who breaks with Communism must break not only with the power of its vision and its faith. He must break in the full knowledge that he will find himself facing the crisis of history, but this time without even that solution which Communism presents, and crushed by the knowledge that the solution which he sought through Communism is evil against God and man. (pp. 191-193)

Bowman (2006) describes its allure in relation to the honor culture it appeared to present:

> Hemingway himself, of course, as well as Orwell and many others ostentatiously went to Spain to fight on the side of the Communists. Part of the reason for the attractiveness of Communism during the 1930s was surely that it offered a version of progressive heroism that was so much in keeping with the predispositions of the postwar generation. No *miles gloriosus*, the Communist hero was instead no more than a Darwinian stepping stone on the way to the radiant future towards which mankind was supposed to be marching in lockstep with Marxian "history." (p. 139)

Lewy (1988) reveals how even the American pacifist movement began to align with violent Communist states:

Over the past twenty years American pacifism has undergone a remarkable transformation. While at one time pacifists were single-mindedly devoted to the principles of nonviolence and reconciliation, today most pacifist groups defend the moral legitimacy of armed struggle and guerilla warfare, and they practice and support the communist regimes emerging from such conflicts. This crucial change in outlook began during the American involvement in Vietnam when the leading pacifist organizations not only opposed the U. S. role but gradually became ardent supporters of the National Liberation Front. This friendly disposition toward so-called national liberation movements has continued—although, significantly, it does not include movements battling communist domination. Few pacifists show any sympathy for the Afghan *mujaheddin* fighting the Russian occupation of their country, for Angola's Unita struggling against Cuban-aided communist rule, or for the various groups opposing the Sandinista regime of Nicaragua...

Whereas in the 1930s and 1940s most American pacifists showed a healthy skepticism about the sincerity of Communist-led peace movements and the political utility of collaborating with them, in recent years pacifist organizations have increasingly abandoned their earlier opposition to a united front with communist groups and their front organizations. This trend began during the 1960s, when the antiwar movement, including its pacifist component, quite deliberately accepted the principle of nonexclusion, which has continued to the present day. (pp. vii-viii)

Catholic teaching knows that the truths of the Church trump those of Communism, as Pius XI (1937) wrote:

> Finally, We know from reliable information that flows into this Center of Christendom from all parts of the world, that the Communists themselves, where they are not utterly depraved, recognize the superiority of the social doctrine of the Church, when once explained to them, over the doctrines of their leaders and their teachers. Only those blinded by passion and hatred close their eyes to the light of truth and obstinately struggle against it. (#35)

Communist influence on most criminals—though some prison/criminal gangs have Communism woven throughout their gang narrative—is surreptitious because by temperament, criminals are conservative, so its influence is hidden under the guise of Liberation Theology, Socialism, or Social Justice, the softer generic terms used by liberal Catholics and non-Catholics.

A counter-intuitive perspective is that much of the intellectual impact of Communism was—and remains—in the West, rather than in Russia (perhaps explaining its recent descent into state criminality) as Laqueur (1994) writes:

> Most Western observers, including the experts among them, overrated the depth of ideological belief inside the Soviet Union. Quite possibly, there were more believers in Marxism in Western academic institutions than in the whole of the Soviet Union. Even among staunch supporters of the regime, Communist doctrine as a source of belief had been replaced by patriotism, or the assumption that the present state of affairs [the 1970s and 1980s] even if unsatisfactory, was preferable to others they could envisage. Or they were motivated by self-interest. For there were millions who had a vested interest in the survival of a regime, which had bestowed on them social status, power (even if only the power of a minor bureaucrat), and material privileges, which they

would not have had otherwise. Very few Soviet citizens believed in all of Soviet ideology; even fewer rejected all of it. Propaganda was all-pervasive, and isolation from the rest of the world was still quite effective. The prevailing attitude was not anti-Communism but indifference—even as the crisis deepened. (pp. 72-73)

What is fairly common among many Communist-inspired groups is the now well-established pattern of propaganda promoting peace and natural political evolution while working for civil war and political revolution; and the great hidden agenda, destruction of the Catholic Church.

Garcia (2009) writing from Brazil:

> In many milieus today it is in fashion to affirm that one is a socialist. This earns the warm applause of the media. But to be a socialist is much more than just a fashion; it is adhesion to a type of religion. I believe that both socialists and communists - with their various degrees of compromise or initiation - belong to a unique sect. It is a revolutionary, atheist, materialist and Hegelian sect whose universal action is turned toward the destruction of Christian Civilization and the Catholic Church....
>
> In the USSR, *nomenklatura* was the word used to designate the highly-placed bureaucrats and elite members of the Communist Party. They formed a privileged philosophical-religious caste and were rewarded or punished insofar as they either adopted or deviated from the tenets of Socialism.
>
> Throughout the world analogous elites control socialist and communist agents who proselytize useful innocents and bring them to their creed. To attract these people, the agents discuss social justice, the distribution of wealth, equality, etc.

> To rise in the ranks of the sect, however, what counts is not adherence to the utopian ideals of the "perfect" society raised in those discussions. Instead, the important factor of selection is to know to what degree a neophyte denies "bourgeois morals," that is, Catholic Morals and Natural Law. If a person does not hesitate to lie, steal, sell his/her body, betray his country and other such immoral things for the advantage of the sect, then he or she is a strong candidate to rise in the sect. (n.p.)

In the West it has been a long-term strategy to reduce the attention paid to Communism by refocusing the attention on the evils of capitalism and, in large part, it has been a successful strategy.

Moynihan (2013) in a book review about the book, *Iron Curtain: The Crushing of Eastern Europe*, by Anne Applebaum, writes:

> Applebaum's book is an important contribution to the literature of Communism. There has long been an ideological campaign—to which Frankel appears committed—to counter the "triumphalist" history of the Cold War (the *Guardian*'s reviewer identifies Applebaum as a "right-wing cold warrior"). As she observes in her introduction, there has been a sustained push by revisionist historians to blame the Cold War's origins not on the genocidal paranoiac Joseph Stalin, but on the inflexible anti-Communist Harry Truman. *Iron Curtain*—along with other, less accessible recent books—nimbly dispatches such theories. (n.p.)

Applebaum's book (2012) is a powerful reminder of the very deep restructuring of the individual psychology of the secret police which Communist governments in Eastern Europe used to control the captured country's population:

The new recruits to the Eastern European secret police services learned espionage techniques, fighting skills, and surveillance methods from the NKVD and later from the Soviet KGB. From their Russian mentors, they also learned how to think like Soviet secret policemen. They learned to identify enemies even where none seemed to exist, because Soviet secret policemen knew the methods enemies used to conceal themselves. They learned to question the independence of any person or group that called itself politically neutral, because Soviet secret policemen did not believe in neutrality.

They were also trained to think in the long term and to identify potential enemies as well as actual opponents of the regime. This was a profoundly Bolshevik obsession. In March 1922, Lenin himself had declared that the "greater the number of representatives of the reactionary clergy and reactionary bourgeoisie we succeed in executing...the better. We must teach these people a lesson right now, so that they will not dare even to think of any resistance for several decades." In an essay written for the benefit of future cadets, one of the Stasi's own historians explained that the organization "from the beginning could not be restricted to defending the attacks of the enemy. It was and is an organ that has to use all means in the <u>offensive fight</u> against the opponents of socialism."

At the same time, Eastern European secret policemen were also taught to feel the Soviet Union's scorn and hatred for those whom it opposed. From the late 1930s, Stalin had begun to refer in public to the USSR's enemies in what one historian has called "biological-hygienic terms." He denounced them as vermin, as pollution, as filth that had to be "subjected to ongoing purification," as "poisonous weeds." Some of that venom is

> echoed in the young Czeslaw Kiszczak's reports from London, quoted earlier: "Those who aren't returning and are staying in England for material reasons would probably render certain services for money, as they are typical products of [prewar] Poland, people without deeper feelings, without ambition and honor."
>
> Finally, the Soviet comrades taught their protégés that anyone who was not a communist was, by definition, under suspicion as a foreign spy. (pp. 84-85)

This deep training and enforcement throughout the Communist dominated countries of Eastern Europe and within Russia itself, is not something that would dissipate over a few years out from under the Soviet yoke, but, as we have learned since, has been usefully brought into service of the criminal state Russia has become.

In the context of the apparition of the Holy Virgin Mother at Fatima (six consecutive monthly apparitions beginning in May, 1917) calling for the consecration of Russia to save the world from the horrors of Communism, and what has happened since, Jesuit Father Edmund Walsh (1928) after extensive travels in and about Russia in the early 1920s, describes what happened there in 1917:

> For Russia not only presents a story that will engage the best historians of the world for generations to come; it is an actual, insistent fact of the present, too. Bolshevism is an international reality which only the hopelessly intransigent can ignore. If the World War did not entirely destroy modern organized society, it assuredly did bring civilization to the crossroads. The victors of the second Russian revolution, that of November 1917, frankly and brutally took the road to the extreme left, driving a weakened, demoralized Russia before

them, calling on stronger nations to follow. That way madness lies, as they have now learned and reluctantly admitted, taught by the inexorable laws of nature operating through economic pressure. *"Drive out Nature with a pitchfork, she will come back every time."* (Horace) But it is my deliberate judgement, based on six years' close observation of European and Russian affairs, that no lasting peace is possible in Europe or Asia until the breach between Russia and the West is securely bridged. For that difference, that breach, is not a chasm dug by national hatred, by historic feud or racial antipathy. One or other of such specific motives made Greeks the natural enemies of Turks, made France distrust Germany, and set Celt against Saxon. But the issue created by the second Russian revolution strikes at the very concept of human society as now organized and proposes an entirely new civilization.

It was not merely a revolution in the accepted sense as historically understood,—that is, a reallocation of sovereignty,—but revolution in the domain of economics, religion, art, literature, science, education, and all other human activities. It sought to create a new archetype of humanity, the "collective man," and a new culture adapted to the impersonal "mass man" who should displace forever "the soul-encumbered individual man." It was meant, and so proclaimed by its protagonists, to be a challenge to the modern State as constituted, not merely in Imperial Russia, but throughout the entire civilized world. It was philosophic materialism in arms, the most radical school of thought that has ever come upon the stage of human affairs. (pp. 5-6)

This prophetic analysis from Fr. Walsh has proven to be very accurate, and the ideal of the revolutionary and pure "collective man" captured many intellectuals in the decades ahead, as it sadly—though under a different name "for the people"—still does today.

Communism, in this context, is the further extension of Nietzsche's Overman, from insane fantasy to insane action.

Laqueur (1994) writes about why many from the West came to love Russia:

> Many of those who went to Moscow and returned idolizing Stalin and his system were politically naïve people who gravitated toward the maintenance of order and other traditional values. The Webbs [Sidney & Beatrice] and Thomas Mann are obvious examples; they could not have supported Russia in the age of Lenin and Trotsky, whereas under Stalin it became considerably easier for them. The great majority of "fellow travelers" were not "intellectual friends of Communism," as some latter-day Western historians tend to believe, but friends of the Soviet Union. This may appear a contradiction in terms, for how could anyone support the Soviet Union without at the same time subscribing to the all-pervasive ideology underlying it? But they could and they did; a division was made between Communist ideology and Soviet achievements. Doctrine was thought to be of relatively little importance.
>
> Some thought that Communism was a reincarnation of progressive Christianity. One example is the "Red Dean" of Canterbury.
>
> Others believe that Stalinism represented a specific Russian road to democracy. Whatever the explanation, it would be difficult to find prominent Western sympathizers who, as the result of visits to Moscow, engaged in a serious study of dialectical materialism, let alone understood and accepted all its tenets. Even Rolland and Feuchtwanger did not

read Lenin and Stalin except perhaps for a few of their speeches. A few of the French and American fellow travelers regarded the Russian Revolution as an extension of the French and American Revolution....

What attracted Western fellow travelers to the Soviet Union? Above all, the apparent decline of the West, as manifested in the Great Depression, and the seeming inability of Western governments to cope with it. Later it was the threat of fascism, and still later the alliance with the Soviet Union in World War II. The growing interest in the Soviet planned economy as a reaction against the failure of irrational and chaotic capitalism has been described in the memoirs of many contemporaries. In Russia, living standards were low, but at least the minimal demands of the people (all people) were fulfilled. No one was unemployed, and the situation was said to improve every year. (pp. 19-20)

The attraction was widespread, as F.A. Hayek writes in the Foreword to the magisterial work, *Socialism*, by Mises (1981):

> When *Socialism* first appeared in 1922, its impact was profound. It gradually but fundamentally altered the outlook of many of the young idealists returning to their university studies after World War I. I know, for I was one of them.
>
> We felt that the civilization in which we had grown up had collapsed. We were determined to build a better world, and it was this desire to reconstruct society that led many of us to the study of economics. Socialism promised to fulfill our hopes for a more rational, more just world. And then came this book. Our hopes were dashed. *Socialism*

> told us that we had been looking for improvement in the wrong direction. (p. xix)

And is it not so always with the young—if certainly was with me—that the allures of idealism, great adventure, and the creation of a heaven on earth, a heaven one can see, touch, really feel, far outweigh the wispy promises about heaven after life; and more, this eternal yearning of the young provides the underpinning of the importance of Catholic evangelism, especially among the young, so well exemplified by World Youth Day.

One of the books which made a huge impression upon these returning idealists who did not read *Socialism*, was *Ten Days That Shook the World*, by John Reed; and its romantic, while still technical, approach fired the spirits of many who would become American Communists.

The cover of the Modern Library 1935 edition of Reed's book notes:

> The breathless story of the Russian Revolution, told by an eye witness and officially approved by Lenin.

The introduction by Granville Hicks notes:

> Yet Reed was not a revolutionary. He voted for Woodrow Wilson in 1916, chiefly, he said, "because Wall Street was against him." At the end of his class report in 1917 he put "Member: Harvard Club, I.W.W.," but he was a member of the I.W.W. because he liked its fighting spirit, its romantic leaders, its exciting songs. He opposed the war, and he knew that it was a capitalist war; he realized that capitalism must sooner or later be superseded; he was willing to help any enemy of capitalism; but he had no concrete plan for the destruction of the existing order and only the vaguest notion of what sort of social system should take its place.

> He had to see for himself, and during the world-shaking ten days he saw. There was never any wavering in Reed's mind after that. He knew that only the proletariat could destroy capitalism, that it must be led by a disciplined party, that it must be prepared to resist the violence of its enemies, and that it must capture the machinery of government and establish a dictatorship. (pages are not numbered but the fourth and fifth of the Introduction)

And Reed (1935) in the 1919 preface, writes:

> It is still fashionable, after a whole year of the Soviet Government, to speak of the Bolshevik insurrection as an "adventure." Adventure it was, and one of the most marvelous mankind ever embarked upon, sweeping into history at the head of the toiling masses, and staking everything on their vast and simple desires. Already the machinery had been set up by which the land of the great estates could be distributed among the peasants. The Factory-Shop Committees and the Trade unions were there to put into operation workers' control of industry. In every village, town, city, district and province there were Soviets of Workers' Soldiers' and Peasants' Deputies, prepared to assume the task of local administration.

> No matter what one thinks of Bolshevism, it is undeniable that the Russian Revolution is one of the great events of human history, and the rise of the Bolsheviki a phenomenon of world-wide importance. Just as historians search the records for the minutest of details of the story of the Paris Commune, so they will want to know what happened in Petrograd in November, 1917, the spirit which animated the people, and how the

> leaders looked, talked and acted. It is with this in view that I have written this book.
>
> In the struggle my sympathies were not neutral. But in telling the story of those great days I have tried to see events with the eye of a conscientious reporter, interested in setting down the truth. (p. xii)

This book and the author's deep influence over the intelligentsia of the early Twentieth Century—captured brilliantly in the insightful docudrama *Reds* in which Warren Beatty plays John Reed, which, by the way, is a very powerful, romantic, and idealistic film—played a substantial role in the Russian Communist penetration into American life.

The importance reached into heaven and the Holy Virgin Mother Mary appeared at Fatima to warn of the results of this event, should the Church—acting through the Holy Father and all of the world's bishops—not consecrate Russia to her Immaculate Heart, which the Church did not and has not, as of this date, done.

There have been many consecrations proclaiming to be in response to Fatima, but virtually none of them mention Russia by name, which were her precise instructions, virtually all are presented as consecrations of the world, and even now one is being planned by Pope Francis, as the Catholic News Agency (2013, August 14) reports:

> VATICAN CITY — Pope Francis will consecrate the world to the Immaculate Heart of Mary Oct. 13 as part of the Marian Day celebration that will involve the iconic statue of Our Lady of the Rosary of Fatima. (n.p.)

Communism in America—as represented by American Communists and a complicit liberal/progressive political community, largely through the representation of former U.S. Senator Joseph McCarthy as an out-of-control, foaming-at-the-mouth political extremist pursuing imaginary enemies—has accomplished the same result as Satan, convincing everyone that he doesn't exist.

What decades of research and new books on Senator McCarthy's accusations that the American government was penetrated by Communists have proven, is that he was absolutely right.

He was certainly a flawed messenger, but his central message was correct.

Marx & Engels (1998) wrote in their magnum opus:

> A spectre is haunting Europe—the spectre of Communism. All the powers of old Europe have entered into a holy alliance to exorcize this spectre: Pope and Tsar, Metternich and Guizot, French radicals and German police spies.
>
> Where is the part in opposition that has not been decried as communistic by its opponents in power? Where the opposition that has not hurled back the branding reproach of Communism, against the more advanced opposition parties, as well as against its reactionary adversaries?
>
> Two things result from this fact:
>
> 1. Communism is already acknowledged by all European powers to be itself a power.
> 2. It is high time that Communists should openly, in the face of the whole world, publish their views, their aims, their tendencies, and meet this nursery tale of the Spectre of Communism with a manifesto of the party itself. (pp. 33-34)

The central fact in the ability of Catholicism to defeat Communism in the conversion of criminals is that the former has walked the talk and the latter has not.

Communism's narrative core is that humanity is composed of economic beings struggling against one another to gain power over others.

Catholicism's narrative core is that humanity is composed of spiritual beings struggling against sin to gain heaven.

At the center of the Communist system is terror and government coercion.

At the center of Catholicism is love and individual choice.

It is easy to see the attraction Communism represents for some criminals to whom money in the hand is far more valuable than a check in the mail, a stolen wallet more joy than a paycheck.

But, ironically, it is easier to prove the truth of Catholicism through its worldly history's congruence with its social teaching, than that of Communism through its worldly history's incongruence with its social teaching.

A recent article by Weigel (2012) reveals the horrible reality of the Chinese Communist regime:

> Uighurs, a Turkish minority living in northwest China, are considered a threat to Chinese ethnic hegemony in the Xinjiang Autonomous Region. Second Uighur children in this lightly populated area are not infrequently euthanized by Han Chinese doctors. Uighur political prisoners are treated by the Chinese government as livestock: not for slave labor, but for organ harvesting. In what became known as the Xinjiang Procedure, high-ranking Chinese government officials needing organ transplants would check into a hospital near a prison where Uighurs were held. Uighur political prisoners were then blood-typed. Blood-typing was followed by tissue-matching. Then, as investigative journalist Ethan Gutmann writes, "the political

prisoner would get a bullet to the right side of the chest. (A Chinese doctor) would visit the execution site to match up blood samples. The officials would get their organs, rise from their beds, and check out."

The Uighurs were not the only victims of this grotesque "procedure." Gutmann estimates that some 65,000 Falun Gong practitioners had their organs "harvested, their hearts still beating, before the 2008 Olympics." An indeterminate number of Chinese House Christians and Tibetans almost certainly suffered the same fate. Something far worse than garden-variety human rights abuse is going on here, Gutmann concludes: "China, a state rapidly approaching superpower status ... has, for over a decade, perverted the most trusted area of human expertise (i.e., medicine) into performing what is, in the legal parlance of human rights, targeted elimination of a specific group" (Ethan Gutmann, "The Xinjiang Procedure," *Weekly Standard*, Dec. 5, 2011).

What kind of regime does these sorts of things? A regime that, to put it gently, lives in a very different moral universe-a moral universe the character and consequences of which Thomas Friedman and other Sinophiles might carefully consider. As, indeed, might the Vatican, where one still finds officials eager to establish diplomatic relations between the Holy See and Beijing. Yet surely the Church's role in any possibly humane Chinese future will be built around its steadfastness under persecution and its forthright defense of the human rights of all (including Uighurs, Tibetans, and Falun Gong devotees), not by reaching agreements with those who may well have harvested organs from Catholic dissidents, pioneering a new form of martyrdom. (n.p.)

The Chinese Communist Party however, has been adroit maintaining another illusion, as McGregor (2010) notes:

> China's post-Maoist governing model, launched by Deng Xiaoping in the late seventies, has endured many attempts to explain it. Is it a benevolent, Singapore-style autocracy? A capitalist development state, as many described Japan? Neo-Confucianism mixed with market economics? A slow-motion version of post-Soviet Russia, in which the elite grabbed productive public assets for private gain? Robber-baron socialism? Or is it something different altogether, an entirely new model, a 'Beijing Consensus', according to the fashionable phrase, built around practical, problem-solving policies and technological innovation?
>
> Few described the model as communist anymore, often not even the ruling Chinese Communist Party itself.
>
> How communism came to be airbrushed out of the rise of the world's greatest communist state is no mystery on one level. The multiple, head-spinning contradictions about modern China can throw anyone off the scent. What was once a revolutionary party is now firmly the establishment. The communists rode to power on popular revulsion against corruption but have become riddled by the same cancer themselves. Top leaders adhere to Marxism in their public statements, even as they depend on a ruthless private sector to create jobs. The Party preaches equality while presiding over incomes as unequal as anywhere in Asia. The communists also once despised the pre-revolutionary comprador class of Chinese businessmen, but rushed without shame

into an alliance with Hong Kong tycoons when taking back the British colony in 1997.

The gap between the fiction of the Party's rhetoric ('China is a socialist country') and the reality of everyday life grows larger every year. But the Party must defend the fiction nevertheless, because it represents the political status quo...

Peek under the hood of the Chinese model, however, and China looks much more communist that it does on the open road. Vladimir Lenin, who designed the prototype used to run communist countries around the world, would recognize the model immediately. The Chinese Communist Party's enduring grip on power is based on a simple formula straight out of the Leninist playbook. For all the reforms of the past three decades, the Party has made sure it keeps a lock-hold on the state and three pillars of its survival strategy: control of personnel, propaganda and the People's Liberation Army. (pp. xii-xiii)

The Church and its doctrine of each life being precious to God, has always been attacked by the world from the day its founder was crucified, and far too often, it has become corrupted in its worldly institutional form, but the corruption by Communism, which the 19th and early 20th century popes had warned about so clearly, seems to have begun in earnest by the failure of the Holy Father to fulfill the command of the Holy Virgin at Fatima in 1917, to consecrate Russia to her Immaculate Heart.

Much of the horrors she foretold which would happen if Russia was not consecrated, have happened.

It is within the diplomacy-influenced reasons partially responsible for that failure—the Russian Orthodox Metropolitan who lobbied to ensure the consecration would not happen, was a KGB directed operative—that we see the Vatican corruption that infected the clear support of Catholic teaching about Communism, rendering it virtually mute.

Amerio (1996) writes about the pact between the Vatican and Moscow regarding Vatican II:

> When one is talking about the liberty of the council, the salient and half secret point that should be noted is the restriction on the council's liberty to which John XXIII had agreed a few months earlier, in making an accord with the Orthodox Church by which the patriarchate of Moscow accepted the papal invitation to send observers to the council, while the Pope for his part guaranteed the Council would refrain from condemning communism. The negotiations took place at Metz in August 1962, and all the details of time and place were given at a press conference by Mgr. Paul Joseph Schmitt, the Bishop of that Diocese [newspaper *Le Lorrain*, 2/9/63]. The negotiations ended in an agreement signed by metropolitan Nikodim for the Orthodox Church and Cardinal Tisserant, the Dean of the Sacred College of Cardinals, for the Holy See. News of the agreement was given in the *France Nouvelle*, the central bulletin of the French communist party in the edition of January 16-22, 1963 in these terms: 'Because the world socialist system is showing its superiority in an uncontestable fashion, and is strong through the support of hundreds and hundreds of millions of men, the Church can no longer be content with a crude anti-communism. As part of its dialogue with the Russian Orthodox Church, it has even promised *there will be no direct attack on the Communist system at the Council.*' On the Catholic side, the daily *La Croix* of February 15, 1963 gave notice of the agreement, concluding: "Following on this conversation, Msgr. Nikodim agreed that someone should go to Moscow carrying

> an invitation, *on condition that guarantees were given concerning the apolitical attitude of the Council.*"

> Moscow's condition, namely that the council should say nothing about communism, was not, therefore, a secret, but the isolated publication of it made no impression on general opinion, as it was not taken up by the press at large and circulated, either because of the apathetic and anaesthetized attitude to communism common in clerical circles or because the Pope took action to impose silence in the matter. Nonetheless, the agreement had a powerful, albeit silent, effect on the course of the Council when requests for a renewal of the condemnation of Communism were rejected in order to observe this agreement to say nothing about it. (Italics in original. pp. 75-76).

This was also written about by Martin (1987) where he uses *Stato* to refer to the Vatican Secretary of State:

> *Stato* reminded his Venerable Colleagues that he had been with the present Holy Father at His Holiness's two meetings with the Soviet negotiator, Anatoly Adamshin, the most recent of which had been earlier this very year of 1981. His Holiness had given the Soviets a guarantee that no word or action, either by His Holiness or the Polish Hierarchy or Solidarity's leaders, would violate the Moscow-Vatican Pact of 1962.

> *Stato* did not need to explain to his listeners that in the late spring of 1962, a certain Eugène Cardinal Tisserant had been dispatched by Pope John XXIII to meet with a Russian prelate, one metropolitan Nikodim, representing the Soviet Politburo of Premier Nikita Khrushchev. Pope John ardently desired to know if the Soviet Government would allow two members of the Russian Orthodox church

> to attend the Second Vatican Council set to open the following October. The meeting between Tisserant and Nikodim took place in the official residence of Paul Joseph Schmitt, then the Bishop of Metz, France. There, Nikodim gave the Soviet answer. His government would agree, provided the Pope would guarantee two things: that his forthcoming Council would issue no condemnation of Soviet Communism or of Marxism, and that the Holy See would make it a rule for the future to abstain from all such official condemnations.
>
> Nikodim got his guarantees. Matters were orchestrated after that for Pope John by Jesuit Cardinal Augustine Bea until the final agreement was concluded in Moscow, and was carried out in Rome, in that Vatican Council as well as in the policies of the Holy See for nearly two decades since. (pp. 85-86)

However, one prominent chronicler of Vatican II, Wiltgen (1985) writes about another version involving a Monsignor rather than a Cardinal:

> When Bishop [Metropolitan] Nikodim met Monsignor Willebrands in Paris in August, 1962, he told him that his Church [Russian Orthodox] would react favorably to an invitation [to Vatican II] if Monsignor Willebrands would go to Moscow and invite Patriarch Alexius personally. This Monsignor Willebrands did, visiting Moscow from September 27 to October 2. He explained the items on the Council agenda to the Patriarch, and issued a verbal invitation. He received no immediate reply, however, because the written invitation had not yet arrived.
>
> The matter of Communism did not come up directly at either the Paris or the Moscow meetings. No request was made by the Russian Orthodox

> Church that the subject should not be treated at the Council, and no assurance was given by Monsignor Willebrands that it would not. In explaining the Council agenda, Monsignor Willebrands simply stated that the problem was treated positively in the Council program. However, he made it clear that, once the Council had opened, the Council Fathers were free to alter the program and introduce any topic they wished. (p. 122)

Also occurring during the 1960's was the notorious meeting—related to that at Metz in refusing to condemn evil—at the Kennedy compound where American Catholic religious leaders developed the strategy for Democratic Catholic politicians to support abortion against the clear teaching of the Church.

Hendershott (2006) writes about the meeting:

> In a long-forgotten meeting at the Kennedy compound in Hyannisport, on a hot summer day in 1964, the Kennedy family and their advisers and allies were coached by leading theologians and Catholic college professors to accept and promote abortion with a "clear conscience." Albert Jonsen, a former Jesuit, recalls how this happened.
>
> > In July, 1964, Jesuit priest, Fr. Joseph Fuchs, renowned Catholic moral theologian and a professor at the Gregorian University in Rome,...and I, the American novice, traveled to Cape Cod to join Catholic theologians, Fr. Robert Drinan, the dean of Boston College Law School; Fr. Richard McCormick, Fr. Charles Curran...
>
> Another Jesuit who helped redefine abortion for the Kennedy family at that meeting in Hyannisport was Fr. Giles Milhaven, who later recalled at a 1984 breakfast meeting of Catholics for a Free Choice:

> The theologians worked for a day and a half among ourselves at a nearby hotel. In the evening we answered questions from the Kennedys and the Shrivers. Though the theologians disagreed on many a point, they concurred on certain basics...and that was that a Catholic politician could in good conscience vote in favor of abortion. (pp. 10-11)

Working from within to corrupt Church teaching was a specialty of Communism and the Communist's work in America began soon after the Russian Revolution, as Romerstein & Breindel (2000) write:

> While the Communists worked hard to help feed the starving Russians, they dreamed of bringing the American people to the glories of living in a Communist society. In 1926, a year after [Whittaker] Chambers joined the Party, the members were proudly wearing a pin which depicted a red hammer and sickle and read, "USSR 9th Anniversary, Forward to the Soviet Republic of the USA," whereas a few years earlier they had hidden their views in the underground. Luckily for them, most Americans didn't even know that they existed.
>
> As Earl Browder, who headed the Party during its heyday in the 1930s, would later boast:
>
>> Entering the 1930s as a small ultra-left sect of some 7,000 members, remnant of the fratricidal factional struggle of the 1920s that had wiped out the old "left wing" of American socialism, the CP rose to become a national political influence far beyond its numbers (at its height it never exceeded 100,000 members), on a scale never before reached by a socialist movement claiming

the Marxist tradition. It became a practical power in organized labour, its influence became strong in some state organizations of the Democratic party (even dominant in a few for some years), and even some Republicans solicited its support. It guided the anti-Hitler movement of the American League for Peace and Democracy that united a cross-section of some five million organized Americans (a list of its sponsors and speakers would include almost a majority of Roosevelt's Cabinet, the most prominent intellectuals, judges of all grades up to State Supreme Courts, church leaders, labour leaders, etc.). Right-wing intellectuals complained that it exercised an effective veto in almost all publishing houses against their books, and it is at least certain that those right-wingers had extreme difficulty getting published.

While Browder's boast contained a lot of truth, he could hardly take full credit. The Communist Party USA only broke out of its isolation in 1935, when the Comintern [*Lenin's Bolsheviks believed that unless socialist revolutions triumphed world-wide, they would be defeated by international capitalism, so they organized the Communist International—abbreviated as Comintern—in Moscow in 1919 to foment revolution around the world.*] taking advantage of the widespread legitimate fear of German Nazism, ordered the international Communist movement to adopt an ecumenical attitude and stretch its hands out to those it previously hated, including socialists and Catholics. (Italicized section added. pp. 98-99)

The work with Catholics appears to have focused to some extent on two major orders of the Church, the Society of Jesus and the Maryknoll Society, as well as the lay Catholic

Worker Movement founded by Dorothy Day and Peter Maurin.

Communist influence on the two orders has been written about by others, but as Dorothy Day is being proposed for sainthood, her movement will be our focus here.

The Catholic Worker Movement remained aligned with Communism in its most central strategy, public control of property, which Miller (1973) the official biographer of Dorothy Day, acknowledges:

> Over the years Dorothy Day and her friends have been accused of harboring a profound naivete on Communism, the other contemporary myth form. To the more choleric, the movement has not only been "soft" on Communism but was its knowing agent. Fundamentally, the two philosophies are profoundly at odds. They are at odds on the question of freedom. For Communism, freedom comes when time's flow is brought into a humane material alignment. The Worker, too, believes in this alignment but not through the instrumentality of force and state organization. The material is the means to transcendence, the means by which man practices his charity, shows his love, and through which in the beauty of nature he can find God. In the Communist sense, it is time that gives to freedom its "tragic principle," and it is divine grace only that can at last bring man through the snare of time. (p. 15)

Dorothy Day, having been a Communist, could have become, after her baptism, a powerful advocate warning of the dangers of Communism; the traditional route taken by former Communists who became Catholic, as part of becoming Catholic is realizing the revealed truth *is* true, rendering all other proclaimed truths false, suspect, wrong; as I have discovered.

Not to act on this and reveal the wrongness of Communism and the rightness of Catholicism, is, almost in itself, proof that she did not find Communism wrong; and in fact, her work throughout her life, remained supportive of Communist positions, leaders, and countries.

Dorothy Day was surely the major Communist-inspired voice in progressive American Catholic circles (often working under the social justice banner) and the Catholic Worker Movement she founded virtually parallels the anti-war, anti-prison, anti-capital punishment mantras which Communist governments working in America advocate, as Miller writes:

> Part of the affront offered by the Worker to the public, but especially to the Catholic public, was its disposition to make common cause with Communists against those actions they mutually opposed, even to the point of speaking of Communists as "brothers," and always insisting, when recognizing the shortcomings of Communism, that those of capitalism were as obvious. "I have spoken," wrote Dorothy Day, "at Carnegie Hall against the Smith and McCarran acts, with Communists, and fellow travelers, others of us have walked on picket lines protesting the payment of income tax…in Peter Maurin's words, 'we have no party line, neither Communist or Catholic.'"
>
> It was about this same time that Dorothy Day, Irene Naughton, and Robert Ludlow published a statement on anti-Communism: "Although we disagree with our Marxist brothers on the question of the means to use to achieve social justice, rejecting atheism and materialism in Marxist thought and in bourgeois thought, we respect their freedom as a minority group in this country….We protest the imprisonment of our Communist brothers and extend to them our sympathy and

> admiration for having followed their conscience even in persecution." (*Ibid.* p. 229)

Working under the social justice mantra is an idea evolving from the Russian Communist and pre-Communist intelligentsia which Banerjee, in a new introduction to the work of Russian philosopher Nikolai Berdyaev (2006) describes:

> With admirable pith and charity, Berdyaev lays bare the poverty and the narrowness of thought embedded in the culture of several generations of Russian radicalism, from Belinsky to the Marxists. He discloses a virulent strain of pseudo-religious beliefs, barely concealed under the professions of atheism that united the various factions of that schismatic sect. The prime example of this is the elevation of the moral imperative of social justice as the highest category of truth *(pravda)*, above and beyond the criteria of intellectual integrity associated with truth as *veritas*. He attributes this root phenomenon to "the orientation of their will," rather than to a defect in thinking. (p. xi)

Berdyaev (1977) elaborates:

> What is most striking is that the attitude toward philosophy was just as crude as was that toward other spiritual values; philosophy has been denied its independent significance and has been subordinated to utilitarian social goals. The exclusive and despotic sway of a utilitarian moral standard; the equally exclusive and oppressive "love for the people" and "love for the proletariat"; the worshipping of "the people," its welfare and interests; and the spiritual depression that results from political despotism have all led to a very low level of philosophic culture among us. Philosophical learning and philosophical development have spread amongst our intelligentsia only to a very

limited extent. High philosophical culture has been restricted to a few individuals, who by this very fact were distinguished from the world of the *intelligentshchina*. It was not simply a matter of our having little philosophical learning—a misfortune that can always be rectified—but our specific mental framework and our specific way of appraising everything were such that genuine philosophy necessarily remained closed and incomprehensible, and philosophical creation seemed a phenomenon of a mysterious other world. Perhaps some have read philosophical books and have understood, superficially, what they have read. But inwardly they have had as little contact with the world of philosophical creation as they have had with the world of beauty. This is to be explained not by any defects of intellect, but by the orientation of their will. That will has created the traditional and unyielding intelligentsia milieu which has absorbed the populist world-view and utilitarian ethic into its flesh and blood, where they persist, in fact, to this very day. (p. 4)

Byrne (2010)—virtually alone with an insightful and penetrating understanding of the deep Communist orientation of this seminal organization and its founders— writes about the Catholic Worker Movement in the introduction to her book:

The Catholic Worker Movement was co-founded by Dorothy Day and Peter Maurin in New York, on 1st May 1933, to provide food, clothing and shelter for the destitute during the years of the Great Depression. It was a movement built on the long-term despair of Americans who turned to radical political and social movements for a solution to unemployment, homelessness and poverty. For Day and Maurin it was an opportunity to fulfil their dream of starting a radical mass movement that might one day reverberate around the world. But in

> the intervening period they devoted their energies to fomenting a revolution against the US government, immersed as it was in upholding all the social and political institutions which they wanted to abolish: Capitalism, industrial corporations, big business and the armed forces. These they regarded as the causes of poverty and injustice in the world.
>
> Key to the technique of protest was to project an image as a victim in the "class struggle" described by Karl Marx, then to seize the moral high ground by attacking the other side as the greedy, guilty "bourgeois." It is essential to keep in mind that Day's theories for a new social order share a common identity: they were all part of a "culture of victimization" which claims that any kind of social disadvantage is due entirely to "oppression" by the "bourgeoisie". That explains her presumption that in the struggle for "liberation" the poor and the workers were by definition always innocent even when they resorted to armed violence, and rich capitalists always the guilty party even when they contributed notably to the common good. (pp. ix-x)

Zwick, M. & L. (2005) notes the importance of the meeting between Dorothy Day & Peter Maurin from the Communist and liberal Catholic's perspective:

> The meeting of Peter and Dorothy brought together two of the most important Catholics of the twentieth century. Catholicism in the United States would be changed forever. (p. 12)

Coulter (2003) describes liberal moral blindness, which helps explain the actions of Dorothy Day, Peter Maurin and the Catholic Worker Movement within the Catholic Church:

Liberals chose Man. Conservatives chose God. The struggle between the two great faiths was the subtext of every great political conflict in America in the second half of the twentieth century. It was this conflict that fueled the Chambers-Hiss hearings, "McCarthyism," Vietnam, Watergate, and the elites' abiding hatred for Ronald Reagan. At the end of the century, and against the odds, the free world won.

It was a crushing defeat for liberals. Not because liberals were necessarily Communists, though many were, but because they had been morally blind to Communism. Democratic administrations contained archipelagos of Communist spies, but Democrats had never, not once, responded with genuine anger to Soviet espionage. Liberal elites defended traitors. In response to the Soviet threat, the Democrats consistently counseled defeat, supplication, and retreat.

Indeed, they spent most of the Cold War jeering at phrases like "Soviet threat." They said Communist advances were inevitable and Communist dictators were "agrarian reformers." No one "lost" China. Détente—not victory—was the best the free world could hope for. Phrases like "captive nations" and "freedom fighters" were invariably put in derisive quotes. As long as the Soviet Union thrived, the "inevitability" argument fell within the range of patriotic behavior. If Soviet domination really was inevitable, liberals were just being brutally frank messengers. But then Reagan won the Cold War. It turned out Communism's triumph wasn't inevitable after all. The left's teleological argument for Communist domination was a lie. Liberals were either dupes or traitors in the greatest battle of the twentieth century. (p. 9)

I think that in Dorothy Day's case, she had conflated Communism with Catholicism so deeply in her own mind and spirit that they were virtually one and the same thing to her—a classic case of being duped—a form of thinking still very prevalent within the Catholic left, especially those still, and they are many, enamored with Liberation Theology.

Now that her cause for sainthood has been approved by the American bishops to move her from the current designation as Servant of God, to the next step in the canonization process, the history of the Vatican's connection to Russian Communism through the period when the Fatima call from the Holy Virgin to consecrate Russia to her Immaculate Heart was not responded to, due, in large part, to the Vatican influence of Orthodox Russian Metropolitans now known to have been KGB directed, will perhaps be examined.

These positions can also be considered to have formed through manipulation by Communist propaganda—especially as in the case of Day's pre-Catholic Worker history of involvement with Communist newspapers and American Communists, representing an extensive background of Communist cooperation—or as Kengor (2010) writes:

> This is a book about dupes, about those Americans who have unwittingly aided some of the worst opponents of the United States. Misled about the true aims of foreign adversaries, many Americans (and other Westerners) have allowed themselves to be manipulated to serve opponent's interests. Most notably, after the Bolshevik Revolution and throughout the Cold War, Communists took full advantage of Western dupes. Indeed, Communist propagandists in the Soviet Union, around the world, and within America itself conducted this duping on a remarkable, deliberate scale and with remarkable, deliberate craftsmanship—with

> America's liberals and progressives as the prime targets. (p. 1)

Catholic social justice is a very good thing, Catholic Communism is not, and the difference is important.

One of the methods used by the Catholic Worker Movement to spread Communist-inspired ideas were their Round Table Discussions, usually led by Peter Maurin, described by long-time Catholic Worker Cort (2003):

> The table was more oval than round, and the discussion was more of a monologue. Peter sat at the head of the table and declaimed one "Easy Essay" after another in his thick French accent—for several hours.
>
> Full as I was of my smart-ass Harvard distinctions, I was anxious to try an essay or two myself or at least ask a few loaded questions. No chance. From long practice on the debating fields of Union Square and Columbus Circle Peter had learned never to breathe between sentences. If by chance he did stop to breathe, he held up a finger to indicate that there was more coming, and if by some act of reckless bravado someone were to ignore the finger and interrupt before Peter was ready to yield the floor, Peter made a face that, like Medusa, was calculated to turn the intruder to stone. (p. 10)

Cort also writes about the different thoughts of Peter Maurin and Dorothy Day, about controlling one's own labor and, in the process, is quite clear about Day's Communism, still disputed by her supporters:

> The practical method for gaining control, or even a meaningful share of control, I thought, was through the trade unions. Here again I clashed with Peter. His gentle but rugged individualism could accept the spiritual discipline of the Catholic Church but

> not the temporal discipline of a trade union. This contradiction was something I could never understand, either on Peter's part or on Dorothy's part: here was a bona fide radical who was antiunion but who, despite that, won the intellectual allegiance of a former Communist like Dorothy, who wrote some of her best pieces in support of the great organizing campaigns of the 1930s and 1940s. (*Ibid.* p. 16)

It doesn't really matter what labels Communist-inspired Catholic social advocates like Dorothy Day use to describe themselves, as the actions they take and the people they chose to be associated with are what determines their character and mission; and by these standards Dorothy Day was a Communist-inspired Catholic working within the Catholic Church promoting people and policies the Catholic Church had declared anathema, just as so many other Communist-inspired Catholics working under the guise of Liberation Theology are doing today.

Pope Leo XIII (1878), in his encyclical warning about Socialism, was clear on the primacy of private property, and the Communist's desire to seize it:

> Lured, in fine, by the greed of present goods, which is "the root of all evils, which some coveting have erred from the faith," they assail the right of property sanctioned by natural law; and by a scheme of horrible wickedness, while they seem desirous of caring for the needs and satisfying the desires of all men, they strive to seize and hold in common whatever has been acquired either by title of lawful inheritance, or by labor of brain and hands, or by thrift in one's mode of life... (#1)

> For, while the socialists would destroy the "right" of property, alleging it to be a human invention altogether opposed to the inborn equality of man, and, claiming a community of goods, argue that

> poverty should not be peaceably endured, and that the property and privileges of the rich may be rightly invaded, the Church, with much greater wisdom and good sense, recognizes the inequality among men, who are born with different powers of body and mind, inequality in actual possession, also, and holds that the right of property and of ownership, which springs from nature itself, must not be touched and stands inviolate. For she knows that stealing and robbery were forbidden in so special a manner by God, the Author and Defender of right, that He would not allow man even to desire what belonged to another, and that thieves and despoilers, no less than adulterers and idolaters, are shut out from the Kingdom of Heaven. (#9)

As stated, one of the vehicles used for Communist penetration of the Church is Liberation Theology and the preferential option for the poor, about which Martin (1987) writes:

> For Marx, the historic task of the proletariat was to struggle against the capitalists and to liberate the people from their oppression.
>
> The "mission" of Liberation Theology, in other words, was Marx's "class struggle." The battle that Liberation Theology told its devotees to fight and to win was not the Ignatian battle of Christ's followers against the Enemy, but the battle of a worldwide class of men and women against the toils and traps of capitalism. As a Liberation Theologian, your "preferential option for the poor" engaged you as a champion of this struggling class. As a Liberation Theologian, your nearest, your most organized, and your most widely spread allies were Communists and Marxists. "The humane face of Marxism," as Teilhard de Chardin had said, promised you "hope of victory." The association of Liberation Theology with Marxists introduced you at once into the one

supreme political issue at stake in our world today: the unending rivalry between the United States and the USSR. Liberation Theology was theology gone geopolitical....

The "preferential option for the poor," for example, as Gutierrez and the others explained it, was based on Christ's own preference for the poor, his preference for the working class versus the rich...

The appealing and even convincing sleight-of-hand here consisted of giving the biblical term *poor* the same meaning as Marx and Marxists had given to the term *proletariat*....

Christ never singled out the proletariat with a preferential option in their favor. Christ acted on no sociological theory about the economic inequality and the political opposition between classes. He aimed at no armed revolution, no political liberation. He had no more preferential option for the poor to the positive exclusion—forcible or otherwise—of the well-off, than he had a preferential option for little children to the exclusion of adults.

Christ's option was for godliness and piety and innocence and humility and fidelity to God's law, wherever he found it—in poor man or rich; in little child or old man; in his rich friends like Nicodemus, Joseph of Arimathea, Lazarus and his two sisters, Mary and Martha; in his poor friends like Zacchaeus, Bartimaeus, the blind beggar or any one of his twelve Apostles. (pp. 309-311)

The Congregation for the Doctrine of the Faith, under Cardinal Ratzinger—now Pope Emeritus Benedict XVI—also addressed Liberation Theology (1986) and regarding the preferential option for the poor, wrote:

Love of preference for the poor

68. In its various forms - material deprivation, unjust oppression, physical and psychological illnesses, and finally death - human misery is the obvious sign of the natural condition of weakness in which man finds himself since original sin and the sign of his need for salvation. Hence it drew the compassion of Christ the Saviour to take it upon himself and to be identified with the least of his brethren (cf. *Mt* 25:40, 45). Hence also those who are oppressed by poverty are the object of a love of preference on the part of the Church, which since her origin and in spite of the failings of many of her members has not ceased to work for their relief, defence and liberation. She has done this through numberless works of charity which remain always and everywhere indispensable. In addition, through her social doctrine which she strives to apply, she has sought to promote structural changes in society so as to secure conditions of life worthy of the human person. By detachment from riches, which makes possible sharing and opens the gate of the Kingdom, the disciples of Jesus bear witness through love for the poor and unfortunate to the love of the Father himself manifested in the Saviour. This love comes from God and goes to God. The disciples of Christ have always recognized in the gifts placed on the altar a gift offered to God himself.

In loving the poor, the Church also witnesses to man's dignity. She clearly affirms that man is worth more for what he is than for what he has. She bears witness to the fact that this dignity cannot be destroyed, whatever the situation of poverty, scorn, rejection or powerlessness to which a human being has been reduced. She shows her solidarity with those who do not count in a society by which they are rejected spiritually and sometimes even

> physically. She is particularly drawn with maternal affection toward those children who, through human wickedness, will never be brought forth from the womb to the light of day, as also for the elderly, alone and abandoned. The special option for the poor, far from being a sign of particularism or sectarianism, manifests the universality of the Church's being and mission. This option excludes no one. This is the reason why the Church cannot express this option by means of reductive sociological and ideological categories which would make this preference a partisan choice and a source of conflict. (#68)

Weigel (1987) writing about Liberation Theology in his seminal book on the political development of the American bishopric, notes:

> Liberation theologies were self-consciously political theologies, and as such could be presented as a necessary corrective to the privatized understandings of Christianity that had long dominated Latin American Catholicism. But most theologians of liberation meant something far beyond deprivatization in their concept of political theology. The Medellin documents demonstrated that a particular politics was being welded to Christian themes and symbols. Development was rejected in favor of revolutionary social change. Consciousness-raising was the essential precondition to such change. Dependency theory explained the cruel realities of Latin American poverty and revealed the equally cruel face of bourgeois liberal capitalism. The essential division in the world was not East/West but North/South, or center-and-periphery. Violence was to be located first in social and economic structures. Moderation was a sign of accommodation and false consciousness. Class struggle was built into the very fabric of social life, and should not be ameliorated,

> but intensified in the minds of the oppressed who would then rise up and throw off the shackles of dependence.
>
> The proximate origin of these themes in Marxism was not denied by liberation theologians, but celebrated. One prominent hierarchical exponent of liberation theology, Archbishop Helder Camara, argued that theologians should "do with Karl Marx what St. Thomas, in his day, did with Aristotle." All of this led to a fascination with and commitment to socialism among theologians of liberation…
>
> In liberation theology, then, Jesus was read, not as the herald and embodiment of the Kingdom of God that transcends all time and every place, but as the liberator who calls us first to social conversion through revolutionary praxis, and who calls his Church to "prophetic denunciation." (p. 288-289)

The founder of Liberation Theology is Fr. Gustavo Gutierrez, (1988) and his book, *A Theology of Liberation*, is the core of the movement; but as he writes in the 15th Anniversary Edition of that book, he has come closer to the Church's definition of Liberation Theology, as entered into the magisterium of the Church by Cardinal Ratzinger of the Congregation of the Doctrine of the Faith in 1984 and 1986—referred to by Gutierrez—than that of Communist-inspired Catholic theologians, some of whom have been silenced by the Church:

> Recent years have witnessed an important debate on the theology of liberation in the context of the Catholic Church. It has meant some painful moments at the personal level, usually for reasons that eventually pass away. The important thing, however, is that the debate has been an enriching spiritual experience. It has also been an opportunity to renew in depth our fidelity to the church in which all of us as a community believe

and hope in the Lord, as well as to reassert our solidarity with the poor, those privileged members of the reign of God. The theological labor must continue, but in pursuing it we now have some important documents of the magisterium that advise us about the path to be followed and in various ways spur us on in our quest. (pp. xviii-xix)

Rather than being a part of the past, as many would have us believe, Liberation Theology is alive and well, as a *US Catholic Interview* (March 2010) with a professor who teaches Liberation Theology, reveals:

Though it grew up in Latin America, liberation theology continues to have lessons for the faithful north of the border.

People who think of "liberation theology" as a 1960's fad should get to know Fordham University Professor Michael Lee, one of a new generation of Catholic theologians.

Lee's faith was transformed when he put it to work among the poor after college, and liberation theology gave him a way to think about his experience. Now he uses it to help undergrads understand the connection between faith and the needs of the world.

"Liberation theology invites people to respond to the gospel in profoundly concrete ways, to establish relationships of solidarity and community," he says. "Faith suddenly makes sense. Christian interaction with the world is richer, more meaningful."

Lee has seen his students' faith become more active in the struggle for justice, even when it comes down to where they buy their clothes, as in the case of the anti-sweatshop movement on college campuses. "Students have been able to question the effects of buying something at Old Navy or the Gap," he says. "And they're just beginning to put the pieces together."

But "liberation spirituality" isn't just for Catholic college students. "We live in an age of globalized technology, communication, and business," Lee says. "People of faith need to reflect on how faith itself is globalized. We can't be ignorant of these places of suffering."

You teach "liberation theology." What exactly is it?

I always start by asking: What does liberation mean? The Second Vatican Council's Pastoral Constitution on the Church in the Modern World, Gaudium et Spes, begins by saying that the joys and hopes, the fears and anxieties of the people of this age, especially the poor, are those of the church. Liberation theology captured the hopes and the longings of poor people, especially in Latin America in the 1960s and 1970s.

I think at the very least liberation theology is a reflection on the fact that human liberation has to be part of the Christian understanding of salvation. Salvation isn't exclusively otherworldly; it has something to do with the here and now. (bolding in original. n.p.)

Many Catholics labeling themselves liberal or progressive who define their work as class struggle and the often needed use of violence to change history, have been caught, and are caught still, by the imagined dreams of Communism—completely blocking the effective reformation of criminals by placing the problem outside instead of inside—so clearly warned against in the 1878 encyclical on socialism by Pope Leo XIII, *Quod Apostolici Muneris*, which opens:

At the very beginning of Our pontificate, as the nature of Our apostolic office demanded, we hastened to point out in an encyclical letter addressed to you, venerable brethren, the deadly plague that is creeping into the very fibres of human society and leading it on to the verge of destruction; at the same time We pointed out also the most effectual remedies by which society might be restored and might escape from the very serious dangers which threaten it. But the evils which We then deplored have so rapidly increased that We are again compelled to address you, as though we heard the voice of the prophet ringing in Our ears: "Cry, cease not, lift up thy voice like a trumpet." You understand, venerable brethren, that We speak of that sect of men who, under various and almost barbarous names, are called socialists, communists, or nihilists, and who, spread over all the world, and bound together by the closest ties in a wicked confederacy, no longer seek the shelter of secret meetings, but, openly and boldly marching forth in the light of day, strive to bring to a head what they have long been planning - the overthrow of all civil society whatsoever...

5. For, indeed, although the socialists, stealing the very Gospel itself with a view to deceive more easily the unwary, have been accustomed to distort it so as to suit their own purposes, nevertheless so great is the difference between their depraved teachings and the most pure doctrine of Christ that none greater could exist: "for what participation hath justice with injustice or what fellowship hath light with darkness?" Their habit, as we have intimated, is always to maintain that nature has made all men equal, and that, therefore, neither honor nor respect is due to majesty, nor obedience to laws, unless, perhaps, to those sanctioned by their own good pleasure. But, on the contrary, in accordance with the teachings of the Gospel, the equality of men consists in this: that all, having inherited the same nature, are called to the same most high dignity of the sons of God, and that, as one and the same end is set before all, each one is to be judged by the same law and will receive punishment or reward according to his deserts. The inequality of rights and of power proceeds from the very Author of nature, "from whom all paternity in heaven and earth is named." But the minds of princes and their subjects are, according to Catholic doctrine and precepts, bound up one with the other in such a manner, by mutual duties and rights, that the thirst for power is restrained and the rational ground of obedience made easy, firm, and noble. (# 1 & 5)

This papal condemnation held for some time, but as Amerio (1996) writes, it withered in the mid-20th Century:

The most outstanding example of this renunciation of Catholic character is that of "Christian Democracy" in Italy, which, although it had been in power for thirty years, gradually weakened its opposition to the socialism and communism the nation had given it an imposing mandate to oppose in the elections of 18 April 1948. A measure of just how bitter the opposition to communism was, and of how grave a danger the country was believed to be facing in 1948, is the fact that even the gates of the most strictly enclosed nuns were unlocked so that the sisters could vote against Hannibal at the gates. In no democratic country in Europe has the change in political climate and social mentality been as radical as in Italy; which is reflected in the fact that the attitude of the party has changed from one of energetic and combative opposition to secularization, to an attitude of acquiescence and accommodation. In 1948 the great goal of the party was the defeat of socialism and communism, but today it is the reaching of an "historic compromise" with the old enemy. (pp. 250-251)

With the Vatican being surrounded by Italian culture and history, it is not surprising that this perspective infiltrated the Church in Rome and eventually, the Church throughout the world.

Being a Communist in a capitalist country gives one a rather glamorous position—especially in glamour-addicted America—of revolutionary; and they are not generally perceived as being connected to the violent and brutal governments led by Communists who use the state power they control to oppress people under the guise of caring for them.

The great enemy of the Church—the prince of this world—has found Communism a worthy tool for many years, continuing today, and Communism's predilection for violence is congruent with his satanic hate of free human beings.

A seminal book on Communism, by Courtois, et al., (1999) notes the tools favored by Lenin:

> Lenin's primary objective was to maintain his hold on power for as long as possible. After ten weeks, he had ruled longer than the Paris Commune, and he began to dream about never letting go of the reins. The course of history was beginning to change, and the Russian Revolution, under the direction of the Bolsheviks, was to take humanity down a previously untraveled path.
>
> Why should maintaining power have been so important that it justified all means and led to the abandonment of the most elementary moral principles? The answer must be that it was the only way for Lenin to put his ideas into practice and "build socialism." The real motivation for the terror thus becomes apparent: it stemmed from Leninist ideology and the utopian will to apply to society a doctrine totally out of step with reality.

In that respect, one may well ask exactly how much pre-1914 Marxism there was to be found in pre-1914 or post-1917 Leninism. Lenin of course used a number of Marxist axioms as the basis for his theories, including the class struggle, the necessity of violence in history, and the importance of the proletariat as the class that brought meaning to history. But in 1902, in his famous address *What is to be Done?* He proposed a new conception of a revolutionary party made up of professionals linked in an underground structure of almost military discipline. For this purpose, he adopted and further developed Nechaev's model [see note], which was quite different from the great socialist organizations in Germany, England, and France.

In 1914 Lenin made a definitive break with the Second International. At the moment when almost all socialist parties, brutally confronted with the power of nationalist sentiments, rallied around their respective governments, Lenin set off on an almost purely theoretical path, prophesying the "transformation of the imperialist war into civil war." Cold reason led him to conclude that the socialist movement was not yet powerful enough to counter nationalism, and that after the inevitable war he would be called on to regroup his forces to prevent a return to warfare. This belief was an act of faith, a gamble that raised the stakes of the game to all or nothing. For two years his prophecy seemed sterile and empty, until suddenly it came true and Russia entered a revolutionary phase. Lenin was sure that the events of this period were the confirmation of all his beliefs. Nechaev's voluntarism seemed to have prevailed over Marxist determinism.

If the prediction that power was there to be seized was correct, the idea that Russia was ready to plunge into socialism, making progress at lightning speed, was radically wrong. And this was one of the most profound causes of the terror, the gap between a Russia that wanted more than anything to be free and Lenin's desire for absolute power to apply an experimental doctrine." (p. 737-738)

[note: Nechaev] Throughout the nineteenth century one section of this revolutionary [Russian Land Movement] movement was linked to violent activity. The most radical proponent of violence within the movement was Sergei Nechaev, whom Dostoevsky used as a model for the revolutionary protagonist of *The Devils*. In 1869 Nechaev published a *Revolutionary Catechism* in which he defined a revolutionary as: a man who is already lost. He has no particular interest, no private business, no feelings, no personal attachments, and no property; he does not even have a name. Everything in him is absorbed by one interest to the exclusion of all others, by a single thought, a single passion...revolution. In the depths of his being, not simply in words but in his actions as well, he has broken all links with society and the world of civilization, with its laws and conventions, with its social etiquette and its moral code. The revolutionary is an implacable enemy, and he carries on living only so that he can ensure the destruction of society. (*Ibid.* p. 730)

This description of the revolutionary is very congruent with that expressed by many professional criminals as a necessary mental and spiritual state to occupy in order to be a successful criminal.

Intellectuals of that time and later were enamoured by the courage and relentlessness of the revolutionary men and women of the early labor union movement of the late 19th century and early 20th, which brought dignity and justice to the workers, power in their labor, and much good to America; but in the latter decades of the 20th century unions became a corrupt force virtually eating its young, degrading the ability of public leadership—once public unions became their major campaign funding source—to provide for the public good without policies being filtered through the demands of public employee unions.

Once the public began to realize that the average pay for public employees demanded by public employee unions was greater than that of the average employee in the private sector, the tide began to turn in the early 21st century, and we are now witnessing the returning of the ability of public leadership to actually work for the public's good rather than the good of the unions.

The strong efforts of the Communist-inspired Catholics—like Dorothy Day and Peter Maurin—and the many sisters and priests who worked with them, to change the social structures of the United States as they have changed the internal structure of the American Catholic Church, continue, and it is strategy most effectively practiced at the local level under the social justice rubric.

McDonough & Bianchi (2002) write:

> One Jesuit, a sixty-eight-year-old writer and artist, reviews the divisions between the Roman authorities and the Society and expresses his admiration for the priority given to social justice by the order but admits that implementation goes slowly:
>
>> "No one should even entertain the idea of women's ordination. Not even the Church can change, etcetera." Rome has made these end runs. There's strong support for conservative Catholics who seem to want Vatican I back again...How does this affect the Society? The Jesuits rarely talk about the latent schism in the church, but they have made an about-face in attitude—"men

> for others" says a great deal. Not the elite avant-garde, the pope's men—rather, service of the poor, the fringe people, an attempt to reshape the structures towards this goal. There have been massive changes in the way Jesuits shape their life and goals, but like an artist moving from one accomplished level to a deeper vision, there's a lot of mud that shows up in the paint, till form has clearly emerged. We're in the mud, period, but there's a light at the end, beginning to emerge.

> The strategy is to pay as little attention as is prudent to what goes on at the command center of the church ("the direction of the institutional church is not the criterion") and to count instead on the grassroots. "There's a revolution going on in the parishes and among the laity." For this Jesuit, the grassroots consists of the parishes, which "need and express what is beyond 'institutions.'" (p. 243)

All of this stems from the ancient sin, that man knows better than God, and for Catholics, who live in the faith whose teachings come from God, and are clearly presented within the two universal Catechisms of the Church, Trent & Vatican II, there is always this authority to seek out when confusion arises, a confusion which the advocates of change driving the social justice movement are deeply enmeshed in.

Holiness for some may be through the Church but for Communist-inspired Catholics who have been trying to redirect the Catholic Church into their very own Kingdom of Heaven on earth for decades; it is through Communism, as noted by Pope Pius XI (1937):

> Thus, aware of the universal desire for peace, the leaders of Communism pretend to be the most zealous promoters and propagandists in the

movement for world amity. Yet at the same time they stir up a class-warfare which causes rivers of blood to flow, and, realizing that their system offers no internal guarantee of peace, they have recourse to unlimited armaments. Under various names which do not suggest Communism, they establish organizations and periodicals with the sole purpose of carrying their ideas into quarters otherwise inaccessible. They try perfidiously to worm their way even into professedly Catholic and religious organizations. Again, without receding an inch from their subversive principles, they invite Catholics to collaborate with them in the realm of so-called humanitarianism and charity; and at times even make proposals that are in perfect harmony with the Christian spirit and the doctrine of the Church. (# 57)

Whether it is the Catholic Worker Movement, Liberation Theology, or the environmental movement, virtually all now linked under the social justice banner, which is a misinterpretation of the true social justice work of the Church as outlined in the *Catechism*:

> **1928.** Society ensures social justice when it provides the conditions that allow associations or individuals to obtain what is their due, according to their nature and their vocation. Social justice is linked to the common good and the exercise of authority.
>
> **1929.** Social justice can be obtained only in respecting the transcendent dignity of man. The person represents the ultimate end of society, which is ordered to him:
>
> What is at stake is the dignity of the human person, whose defense and promotion have been entrusted to us by the Creator, and to whom the

> men and women at every moment of history are strictly and responsibly in debt.

> **1930.** Respect for the human person entails respect for the rights that flow from his dignity as a creature. These rights are prior to society and must be recognized by it. They are the basis of the moral legitimacy of every authority: by flouting them, or refusing to recognize them in its positive legislation, a society undermines its own moral legitimacy. If it does not respect them, authority can rely only on force or violence to obtain obedience from its subjects. It is the Church's role to remind men of good will of these rights and to distinguish them from unwarranted or false claims." (*Catechism of the Catholic Church,* 2nd Edition (1997) #1928-1930)

The Communist-inspired movements want to *mandate* social justice through legislative fiat enforced by governmental power, while Catholic social justice is *proposed* to men and women of good will as the preferred way, the way Christ taught us to live and to treat each other.

The social justice mantra, while particularly attractive for its focus on helping the poor, may be incorrectly presented, as noted by Rose (2013, April 1):

> I think it is fair to say that social justice advocacy is now generally taken to be the idea that there are things that are unjust about free market societies, so we are morally required to attempt to redress these problems. Social justice advocacy, if it is to have any normative meaning, is about what must be done to right these wrongs. Among other things, social justice advocates endorse the exercise of government power to redistribute wealth/income and to regulate behavior to produce a more just

outcome across the whole of society. People drawn from a very wide variety of ideologies and political views would agree with this characterization of the practical meaning and effect of social justice theory regardless of how it is defined.

But is the premise actually true? Do free market societies inevitably produce unjust outcomes, or are social justice theorists incorrectly inferring injustice from what is actually innocuous inequality? In my view the latter is true and the former is false, so social justice theory amounts to a solution in search of a problem. As such, it constitutes a massive straw man argument against the free market society. Making matters worse, it is a particularly attractive straw man argument because it comports well with incorrect but very plausible folk wisdom about what a market economic system is and how it functions. (n.p.)

The 1920s and 1930s were the periods when the Russian Revolution spread its wings, certain of world revolution, and in that expansion, the use of the great lie was advocated—speak to others in their language, hide your true intentions, speak of peace and love while excusing violence and advocating class hatred.

Propaganda became an art form and the Russian Communists and German Fascists became its greatest artists in those horrific decades.

A classic example—and a central plank in Catholic social justice—is the political utility of advocating pacifism.

The intellectual basis of American Catholic pacifism has never been developed appropriately—primarily because it cannot stand up to a rigorous examination through the lens of Aquinas-inspired Catholic teaching—and remains primarily a political stance embraced by the Catholic left, as Weigel (1987) notes:

American Catholicism had been touched by pacifism before Vatican II, most notably by the Catholic Worker movement and the writings of Gordon Zahn. But in the postconciliar period, a renascent American Catholic pacifism stood, not on the margins of the debate over war and peace, but close to its very center. Several factors were responsible for this signal development.

First, one must acknowledge the cumulative impact of the Catholic Worker movement and Dorothy Day, not only in terms of their witness to the whole Church, but also because of the network of relationships that tied the Worker movement into increasingly influential American Catholic thought and action centers....

Despite the emergence of a profoundly felt pacifist conscience in American Catholicism since Vatican II, that conscience has yet to be given a sophisticated theological and political-philosophical explication. Zahn's writings come closest to this standard, but even Zahn was unwilling, perhaps unable, to distinguish between a principled pacifism and a pacifism that had become dominated by New Left currents of thought and styles of political action during Vietnam. Nor was Zahn, or any other American Catholic pacifist theorist, able to argue persuasively the moral requirement of pacifism in a non-pacifist world. The call to personal conversion at the heart of the new American Catholic pacifism makes powerful claims on individual consciences. But it remains to be shown how such an act of conversion can be expected of a government that has the *moral* responsibility of providing for its citizen' security in a persistently violent world.

> These intellectual weaknesses in the pacifist case had disturbing results in American Catholicism.
>
> There was the problem of selectivity—that is, a pacifism applied to American military action or programs, but not to revolutionary violence in the name of "liberation." (pp. 243-246)

Moral blindness formed the foundation upon which the revolutionary violence of Liberation Theology—shaped by Communist theory and practice—grew within the Church and, which still exerts substantial control over the strategies of many religious orders and members of the laity, as well as Catholic organizations.

Another plank in the Catholic Left's vision of social justice is the prison abolition movement, whose roots are based in Communist ideology of state control of production and the mass distribution of wealth to ensure all are well-fed, housed and otherwise taken care of; social goals devoutly to be wished by all Catholics but properly to be manifested through capitalism and the generosity of the charitable impulse.

The prison abolition movement is summarized by Wikipedia:

> The prison abolition movement seeks to abolish prisons and the prison system. The movement advocates for the abolition of prisons and the prison system on the basis of it being ineffective. Prison abolitionists present a broad critique of the modern criminal justice system, which they believe to be racist, sexist, and classist. They also see prisons and the prison system as an ineffectual way to reform criminals, decrease crime, and reconcile the victims of crime. For the prison abolition movement, the goal is not to

improve the system or offer reforms, but to actually shrink the system into non-existence.

Retrieved August 22, 2012 from http://en.wikipedia.org/wiki/Prison_abolition_movement

Undergirding virtually all of the Liberation Theology work emanating from Catholics influenced by Dorothy Day and the Catholic Worker Movement, is the idea of helping others freely, requiring nothing from them save their need, the no-means-test approach to charitable action.

This approach, while having a Catholic history, is not congruent with America's founding principles, as noted by Friedman and McGarvie (2003) writing about charity in early New England:

> New Englanders did worry that generous aid to the poor might actually encourage dependence and idleness. That was, in fact, an important item in the brief English Protestants drew up against the Catholic Church. "The poor ye shall always have with ye": Jesus' dictum had been woven into the fabric of Christianity for centuries. In that faith, medieval churchmen regarded the poor as instruments of providence: their misery ordained to stir feelings of compassion, their sufferings acts of charity. To fulfill this design, the rich were enjoined to give freely to the beggar at their door. Such good works would win renown in this world and credit in the next. The trouble was that alms were bestowed indiscriminately on the virtuous and vicious alike. To the Puritans, "beggars commit sacrilege who abuse the name of Christ, and make their poverty a cloak to keep them idle." It was thus imperative to separate the worthy from the unworthy poor. The former—the aged, the widow, the orphan, the disabled—were victims of circumstances beyond their control; anyone, at any time, could suffer their

> fate, and they deserved the aid of the community. By contrast, the second class had brought on its plight by idleness and intemperance; it was unworthy of public support. This moral distinction, built into the English Poor Law, was carried over to Massachusetts Bay. (p. 34)

During the colonial period, when America's methods of charitable help to the unfortunate were being set into the American character, building or rebuilding the character of the unfortunate not considered worthy of freely given help was essential, as Olasky (1992) writes:

> This early American model also emphasized hospitality, particularly the opening of homes to those suffering destitution because of disaster...Those who made room for widows and orphans often received compensation for out-of-pocket expenditures from town councils of other community organizations.
>
> The model also insisted on "decent living" on the part of those who were helped. (p. 7)

Congruent with this tradition, the great American philanthropist Andrew Carnegie, (1998) whose model for gifting is still being used, wrote:

> Those who would administer wisely must, indeed, be wise; for one of the serious obstacles to the improvement of our race is indiscriminate charity. It were better for mankind that the millions of the rich were thrown into the sea than so spent as to encourage the slothful, the drunken, the unworthy. Of every thousand dollars spent in so-called charity today, it is probable that nine hundred and fifty dollars is unwisely spent—so spent, indeed, as to produce the very evils which it hopes to mitigate or cure....

> In bestowing charity, the main consideration should be to help those who will help themselves; to provide part of the means by which those who desire to improve may do so; to give those who desire to rise the aids by which they may rise; to assist, but rarely or never to do all. Neither the individual nor the race is improved by almsgiving. (pp. 21-22)

Fortunately, this directing of charitable help to those who would help themselves still resonates among many in the private philanthropic class, though government unwisely still administers aid recklessly and often to the detriment of the people it claims to be helping.

There is a virtual library of books written on the corrosiveness of the billions of dollars spent by government in pure welfare with little regard for stimulating self-help.

Communism & Fatima

Fatima was the most important event of the 20th Century and beyond, as Martin (2013, April) notes:

> Fatima was not just the event of the century but an event matchless and timeless, a majestic witness testifying with elemental power about the will of Heaven and the future of earth. It spoke in the fire of the sun and in the gentle words of the Virgin Mary, and promised a surpassing mercy even as it provided a terrifying vision of souls tossed about in the flames of Hell. It set forth conditions for the world's deliverance from an imminent darkness that would be shaped and spread by the Russian followers of Karl Marx. Finally, it assured us that if the Church met those conditions, there would come unimaginable miracles: a converted Russia, a period of peace, and a world in which the beauty of holiness would be honored in a magnificent new way in the person of Mary. And all this was not a fairy tale but truth—a dazzling revelation that both Rome and the dedicated faithful must yet come to fully appreciate, believe in, and live out if the epic event we call Fatima is to fulfill its glorious promise. (pp. 22-23)

However, the shepherds of the Church failed Our Lady and our Church then and continue that failure today.

They not only failed to protect our Church from the Communist wolves, but in all too many cases, became Communist wolves themselves.

The speculation surrounding why the appearance of the Holy Mother and her plea to consecrate Russia to her

Immaculate Heart, has not been followed; continues to this day as Johnston (1980) writes:

> And on 13 June 1929 she [Lucia] received the greatest of all her visions which was only made public in August 1967 after Pope Paul's visit to Fatima. It was a climatic vision of the Most Holy Trinity in which Our Lady came to fulfill her promise of 13 July 1917: "I shall come to ask for the consecration of Russia to my Immaculate Heart." The following is Lucia's own account of that sublime vision, which she wrote in 1931 on the order of her confessor...
>
> "Our Lady then said to me: 'The moment has come for God to ask the Holy Father to make, in union with all the bishops of the world, the consecration of Russia to my Immaculate Heart. He promises to save Russia by this means. There are so many souls that the justice of God condemns for sins committed against me, that I have come to ask for reparation. Sacrifice yourself for this intention and pray.' I gave an account of this to my confessor and he asked me to write down what Our Lord wanted to be done.
>
> "Later on, through an intimate communication, Our Lord complained: 'They have not chosen to heed my request...As the King of France, they will regret it and then will do it, but it will be late. Russia will already have spread her errors throughout the world, provoking wars and persecutions against the Church. The Holy Father will have much to suffer. (pp. 86-87)

The request for the Collegial Consecration was first promised before the Bolsheviks overcame Russia and her Catholic monarchy, eventually killing the entire family of Czar Romanov, and specifically called for later, and it is still unfulfilled.

Part of the reason—the influential power of human relationships—has been uncovered, as Weigel 2010) notes:

> On September 5, 1978, the new pope [John Paul I] received [Russian Orthodox] Metropolitan Nikodim of Leningrad, one of the six presidents of the World Council of Churches and a man who struck many Westerners as deeply pious. The KGB knew Nikodim as ADAMANT, as it knew his secretary, Nikolai Lvovich Tserpitsky (code name VLADIMIR). At the end of his private audience with John Paul, ADAMANT suffered a massive heart attack and died in the Pope's arms. John Paul I later remarked that Nikodim had spoken "the most beautiful words about the Church I have ever heard" during their meeting; his last words, as the Pope held the fallen bishop, were said to have been "I am not a KGB agent." But he was. (p. 99)

Russian Communism's penetration and attempt to control Catholic strategy continued through the papacy of John Paul II, as Weigel writes:

> The search for truth was essential to man, the Pope concluded [John Paul II's address to the United Nations General Assembly October 2, 1979]. Believers and nonbelievers ought to be able to agree on this as a common matter of humanistic conviction.
>
> The Central committee of the Soviet Communist Party might not agree on that. It did agree, however, that something had to be done about John Paul II. Six weeks after the pope spoke at the UN, the Central committee Secretariat issued an "absolutely secret" decree, entitled "On measures of Opposition to the Politics of the Vatican in Relation to Socialist Countries." This was a political document, assigning tasks to different organs of Soviet state power: the various propaganda, radio,

television, and press organs; the Soviet Communist Party's international department; the Soviet Council of Religious Affairs; and the Central committee's Academy of Social Sciences. Each of these instruments of the Soviet state was to do its own distinct work in combating the "perilous tendencies in the teaching of Pope John Paul II," which were to be "condemned in proper form." The decree was signed by the party's chief ideologist, Mikhail Suslov, and was accompanied by several analyses of the situation, including a memorandum, "On the Socio-Political and Ideological Activities of the Vatican on the Contemporary Stage," that was prepared by the KGB, although nominally authored under the auspices of the Council of Religious Affairs....at the same time as the decree was issued, the "KGB was instructed...to embark on active measures in the West" aimed at frustrating the designs of John Paul II and demonstrating that his efforts were a danger to the Catholic Church. "Active measures" in this context would have included propaganda, disinformation campaigns, blackmail, and other tactics as required, with special focus on persuading the world media that John Paul II was a threat to peace. (*Ibid.* pp. 114-115)

Sciabarra (1995) provides some insight into the cultural history that led the Russian Orthodox Church to work so closely with the Communist state:

> The movement toward dialectical transcendence of opposites is manifested especially in the 1840s in Khomyakov's critique of Western religion. Alexy Khomyakov embraced the Slavophile devotion to Orthodox Christianity and personal mystical experience. He viewed Russian Orthodoxy, with its Byzantine roots, as the reconciliation of Catholicism and Protestantism. N.O. Lossky, [Ayn] Rand's teacher and author of the indispensible

> *History of Russian Philosophy,* explains that for Khomyakov, "the rationalism of Catholicism which established unity without freedom gave rise, as a reaction against it, to another form of rationalism— Protestantism which realizes freedom without unity." Khomyakov saw the necessity for a communal, conciliar unity that transcended the Catholic emphasis on the individual judgment of the pope and the Protestant emphasis on the individual judgment of the believer. Russian Orthodoxy bound the Church and the state much more closely than was the case in the West. It was the original organic union, in Khomyakov's view, a freedom-in-unity and a unity-in-freedom. (pp. 26-27)

The Russian Communist presence within the Vatican appears to have been the mortar that kept the Vatican from ever—to this day—fulfilling the wishes of the Holy Mother at Fatima; a tragic conclusion written about by Kramer (2010):

> The subversion of the Orthodox Church by Stalin is certainly among the developments in Russia foreseen by the Virgin of Fatima. This is precisely why She came to call for the consecration of Russia to Her Immaculate Heart; so that Russia would embrace the one true religion and the one true Church, not the schismatic Orthodox Church which was founded in human rebellion against Rome when it left the Mystical Body of Christ over 500 years ago, and thus was constitutionally incapable of avoiding its total Adaptation to Stalinism.
>
> The Orthodox Adaptation began officially when the Metropolitan Sergius of the Russian Orthodox Church published an "Appeal" in *Isvestia* on August 9, 1927…

This, then, is what the Adaptation involved: The church would be silent about the evils of the Stalinist regime. It would be silent in the presence of the Party Line being broadcast and rebroadcast again and again. It would become a purely "spiritual" community "in the abstract", would no longer voice opposition to the regime, would no longer condemn the errors and lies of Communism, and would thus become the Church of Silence, as Christianity behind the Iron Curtain was often called....

Meanwhile, the Church of Silence, in effect, was transformed into an organ of the KGB. Stalin decimated the Russian Orthodox Church; all of the real Orthodox believers were sent off to concentration camps or executed and replaced by KGB operatives.

Shortly before Talantov died in August of 1967, he wrote as follows about the Adaptation:

> The Adaptation to atheism implanted by Metropolitan Sergius has concluded (been completed by) the betrayal of the Orthodox Russian Church on the part of Metropolitan Nikodim and other official representatives of the Moscow Patriarch based abroad. This betrayal irrefutably proved the documents cited must be made known to all believers in Russia and abroad because such an activity of the Patriarchate, relying on cooperation with the KGB, represents a great danger for all believers. In truth, the atheistic leaders of the Russian people and the princes of the Church have gathered together against the Lord and his Church.

Here Talantov refers to the same Metropolitan Nikodim who induced the Vatican to enter into the

> Vatican-Moscow Agreement, under which the Catholic Church was forced to remain silent about communism at Vatican II. Thus, *the same Orthodox prelate who betrayed the Orthodox Church was instrumental in an agreement by which the Catholic Church was also betrayed.* At Vatican II certain Catholic churchmen, cooperating with Nikodim, agreed that *the Roman Catholic Church, too, would become a Church of Silence.* (Italics in original, pp. 108-109)

No matter how many times I read this, I am still shocked that it happened and has been so completely documented from so many sources, yet so completely absent within the perspective of the Catholic public.

Communism, being able to accomplish this powerful strategy against critiques from the one force on earth with the spiritual authority to be heard and to combat it, thus proved itself a very powerful and effective adversary.

Communism is a religion, its bible is *The Communist Manifesto*, its theologians are Lenin, Stalin, Mao, Debray, Fanon; its priests are legion, and its shock troops are too often criminals, harking to the first name of the organization Communism's founders, Marx and Engels, joined:

> In the spring of 1847 Karl Marx and Frederick Engels agreed to join the so called League of the Just, an offshoot of the earlier League of the Outlaws, a revolutionary secret society formed in Paris in the 1830s under French Revolutionary influence by German journeymen—mostly tailors and woodworkers—and still mainly composed of such expatriate artisan radicals. The League, convinced by their 'critical communism', offered to publish a Manifesto drafted by Marx and Engels as its policy document, and also to modernize its organization along their lines. Indeed, it was so

> reorganized in the summer of 1847, renamed League of the Communists, and 'committed to the object of 'the overthrow of the bourgeoisie, the rule of the proletariat, the ending of the old society which rests on class contradictions and the establishment of a new society without classes or private property. (Marx & Engels (1998). (p. 3)

Cummins (1994) writes about the deepening of criminal involvement in Communist revolution through the ideas and writings of the radical elements of the California criminal/carceral movement:

> The prison movement had spun away from its union-building phase. In 1972 the National Lawyers Guild reaffirmed once again the leadership of revolutionary convicts and repeated its faith that they would soon make their break to the streets to raise the level of struggle: "Prisoners are the revolutionary vanguard of our struggle. When prisoners come out, they will lead us in the streets." (p. 221)

Russia's continued domination of the Russian Orthodox Church is reported by Young (2013):

> The biggest news story out of Russia in 2012 was not Vladimir Putin's return to the presidency in May. It was the trial of three young women from the guerrilla-girl punk band Pussy Riot, charged with "hate-motivated hooliganism" for a protest performance in a Moscow church. The women's offense was a brief song-and-dance act at the Cathedral of Christ the Savior in February, opening with a prayer chant of "Mother of God, Blessed Virgin, drive out Putin." On August 17, after a nonjury trial in which the judge blatantly favored the prosecution, Maria Alekhina, Nadezhda Tolokonnikova, and Yekaterina Samutsevich were found guilty and handed two-year prison sentences.

In October, two of the women were transported to remote penal colonies.

The prosecution, which was condemned by figures ranging from German Chancellor Angela Merkel to Icelandic singer Bjork to Polish former president and dissident Lech Walesa, became an international symbol of the Kremlin's heavy-handed approach to dissent and artistic freedom. Yet at its core, the Pussy Riot case was also about the unholy union of organized religion and authoritarian state in modern-day Russia.

Pussy Riot's protest song was about not just Putin but also the cozy ties between the Kremlin and the Russian Orthodox Church under the leadership of the pro-Putin Patriarch Kirill. The indictment against the punk rockers accused them not only of demeaning the beliefs of Orthodox Christians but of "belittling the spiritual foundations of the state."

The case looked and felt like something out of the Dark Ages. The state-run Rossiya television channel repeatedly referred to the women as "blasphemers," while a co-founder of the semi-official pro-Kremlin youth group Nashi warned that the decline of harsh blasphemy laws throughout Europe had set the continent on a path to destructive liberalism. During the trial, the judge deemed it relevant that the Pussy Rioters had violated rules established by an eighth-century church council. Outside the courtroom, the lawyer for one of the prosecution witnesses told a newspaper, with no trace of humor, that the group's actions stemmed from Satan himself. (n.p)

The Holy Mother at Fatima also knew about the real criminal danger of an unconsecrated Russia, due to the crimes—though of a much less magnitude of national violence and brutality than the horror of the Nazi holocaust and the Stalinist terror—which have resulted via a worldwide explosion of organized crime emanating from Russia, as Sterling (1994) writes:

> Organized crime was transformed when the Soviet Empire crashed, and with it a world-order that had kept mankind more or less in line for the previous half-century. As the old geopolitical frontiers fell away, the big crime syndicates drew together, put an end to wars over turf, and declared a *pax mafiosa*. The world has never seen a planetwide criminal consortium like the one that came into being with the end of the communist era.
>
> Perhaps something like it would have come sooner or later anyway. Most of the big syndicates had worked with one or more of the others for years, the Sicilian Mafia with all of them. But the opportunities opening up for them in 1990 were immense—fabulous—and they responded accordingly.
>
> International organized crime, an imaginary menace for many in 1990, was a worldwide emergency by 1993. The big syndicates of East and West were pooling services and personnel, rapidly colonizing Western Europe and the United States, running the drug traffic up to half a trillion dollars a year, laundering and reinvesting an estimated quarter trillion dollars a year in legitimate enterprise. Much of their phenomenal growth derived from the fact that they had the free run of a territory covering half the continent of Europe and a good part of Asia—a sixth of the earth's land mass, essentially ungoverned and unpoliced.
>
> The whole international underworld had moved in on post-communist Russia and the rest of the ex-Soviet bloc: raced in from the day the Berlin Wall

> fell. Where Western governments tended to see Russia as a basket case, the big syndicates saw it as a privileged sanctuary and a bottomless source of instant wealth.
>
> Russia had a runaway black market, a huge potential for producing and moving drugs, an enormous military arsenal, the world's richest natural resources, and an insatiable hunger for dollars of whatever provenance. Furthermore, it had a rampant mafia of its own, in need of Western partners to make the most of these prospects. (p. 14)

Control of Russian culture by organized crime after the fall of Communism is also written about by Satter (2003):

> The victory over communism was a moral victory. Millions took to the streets not because of shortages but in protest over communism's attempt to falsify history and change human nature. As a new state began to be built, however, all attention shifted to the creation of capitalism and, in particular, to the formation of a group of wealthy private owners whose control over the means of production, it was assumed, would lead automatically to a free-market economy and a law-based democracy. This approach, dubious under the best of conditions, proved disastrous in the case of Russia because, in a country with a need for moral values after more than seven decades of spiritual degradation under communism, the introduction of capitalism came to be seen as an end in itself.
>
> The young reformers were in a hurry to build capitalism, and they pressed ahead in a manner that paid little attention to anything except the transformation of economic structures. "The calculation was sober," said Aliza Dolgova, an expert on organized crime in the Office of the

General Prosecutor; "create through any means a stratum in Russia that could serve as the support of reform...All capital was laundered and put into circulation. No measures of any kind were enacted to prevent the legalization of criminal income. No one asked at [privatization] auctions: Where did you get the money? Enormous sums were invested in property, and there was no register of owners. A policy similar to this did not exist in a single civilized country."

The decision to transform the economy of a huge country without the benefit of the rule of law led not to a free-market democracy but to a kleptocracy that had several dangerous economic and psychological features.

In the first place, the new system was characterized by bribery. All resources were initially in the hands of the state, so businessmen competed to "buy" critical government officials. The winners were in a position to buy the cooperation of more officials, with the result that the practice of giving bribes grew up with the system.

Besides bribery, the new system was marked by institutionalized violence. Gangsters were treated as normal economic actors, a practice that tacitly legitimated their criminal activities. At the same time, they became the partners of businessmen who used them as guards, enforcers, and debt collectors.

The new system was also characterized by pillage. Money obtained as a result of criminal activities was illegally exported to avoid the possibility of its being confiscated at some point in the future. This outflow deprived Russia of billions of dollars that were needed for its development. (pp. 1-2)

Lucas (2012) also wrote about the criminal development of post-Communist Russia:

> In no other country have gangsterdom and state power overlapped to such a threatening extent. The most powerful drug cartels may have high-tech communications equipment or the ability to penetrate a law-enforcement agency, or have some politicians on the payroll. But they have nothing that (yet) matches Russia's ruling criminal syndicate's capabilities. It has almost limitless money, global geographical scope and the full armory of state technical and logistical resources, from spy satellites to submarines, giving unprecedented capabilities in snooping and manipulation. Russia's world-class hackers, for example, work sometimes in government, sometimes under official protection and sometimes entirely in their own criminal interest. Russian dirty money and underhand business practices taint and corrode the financial systems, business cultures and politics of the countries they touch. As Don Jensen, a stalwart American critic of the regime, points out, Russia's main export is not oil and gas. It is corruption. (p. 79)

The Marxist infiltration of Catholicism began in Europe, and after the years of occupation by the Nazis and the Communists, which solidified their atheistic ideology within an oppressed European peoples where the ambitious and unscrupulous assumed positions of cultural superiority because of their lack of religious commitment to martyrdom, which most of us can relate to—nor do I remove myself from being uncertain how I would react to live peacefully within an atheistic and immoral Communist culture.

Some in the traditional wing of Catholicism—of which I am somewhat partial to, and I will explain the 'somewhat'—believes the solution to Modernism, of which Communism can be considered as an aspect, is a reassertion of Christendom; the time when European governments—all of which were monarchial—accepted the kingship of God and his vicar, Peter.

The problem here, the 'somewhat', is that a central element of God's plan—until he comes again—is the reign over earth (but not human souls) by Satan, the prince of this world; whose blandishments the Christian way of life is protection against.

Understanding all of this, coming to terms with history and the various blandishments offered by all sides in the Catholic versus Communism debate requires a process of spiritual maturation too few of us reach for.

Maturing in God, is a process each of us has to go through if we are to become mature Catholics, leaving the primitive and childish things like Liberation Theology and Communism behind, and part of this maturation is growing in wisdom and knowledge through the studying of human life on earth through the lens of Catholic doctrine.

About this maturation, Sheed (1946) writes:

> God knew what He would do, but He would not do it yet. "In the dispensation of the fullness of times,: St. Paul tells the Ephesians (1.10), "God was to re-establish all things in Christ." What does "the fullness of times" mean? At least it means that the Redemption was to take place not at a moment arbitrarily chosen, as though God suddenly decided that the mess had gone on long enough and He had better do something about it. There was a fullness of time, a due moment. Looking at it from our angle, we feel it fitting that God did not heal the disease all at once; a disease should run its course. There is a rhythm of sin, as of revolution. Mankind had started on the road of self-assertion; it must be allowed to work out all the bleak logic of self-

> assertion to discover for itself all the unwholesome places into which self-assertion could take it. To be redeemed instantly might have left a faint "perhaps" to trouble mankind's peace; the Devil had said that we should be as gods—perhaps if we had been allowed to try it out thoroughly, we might have become as gods. Well, we were allowed to try it out thoroughly; and we did not become as gods. When mankind knew at last and beyond a doubt that the game was up, might not that have been "the fullness of time"? Certainly there is an element of that in it. St. Paul perhaps is only putting the same idea more positively when he speaks of mankind as growing up, coming to maturity. By sin, mankind threw away the maturity God had conferred upon it, started it off with, so to speak. It had gone after a childish dream and must now go through all the pains of growing back to the maturity it had lost. It would be an element in that attained maturity to know that the dream was childish, to be prepared to put away the things of a child. (pp. 172-173)

Is this not the wonderful way of divine parentage, which we as humans so often strive to attain in our childraising?

Rebellion and questioning authority are congruent with youth, then as now, and for those of us whose youth was influenced by the siren calls of the rebellion prevalent in our youth, the critical examination of the avatars of our youth is always both difficult and exciting; difficult as it shreds a passion of youth, exciting because it presages the wisdom of age.

And so it is for me, writing about Communism, whose Marxist roots briefly influenced my work in prison and for a time after being released.

Conclusion

The great movement after World War II which began to address the huge impact Communism had made within the academy, government, and media, so exemplified by the investigations of Senator Joseph McCarthy; was initially and very successfully represented as a national aberration that had no basis in truth, but which, after the slow release of files from the fall of Soviet Communism, was seen to be, not an aberration, but a valiant effort by heroic people, like Senator McCarthy, to save their country from Communism.

Contrast Communism with Capitalism, as one of Capitalism's fiercest proponents, Ayn Rand (1966), who escaped Communist Russia, and, while vehemently not Catholic, yet proclaimed the nature of economic freedom in terms congruent with Catholic social teaching:

> *Capitalism is a social system based on the recognition of individual rights, including property rights, in which all property is privately owned.*
>
> The recognition of individual rights entails the banishment of physical force from human relationships: basically, rights can be violated only by means of force. In a capitalist society, no man or group may *initiate* the use of physical force against others. The only function of the government, in such a society, is the task of protecting man's rights, *i.e.*, the task of protecting him from physical force; the government acts as the agent of man's right of self-defense, and may use force only in retaliation and only against those who initiate its use; thus the government is the means of placing the retaliatory

use of force under *objective control.* (Italics in original, p. 11)

The ideology of Communism is the ideology of the left, and as we have seen, it is potent, as Collier & Horowitz (1996) write:

> Every movement of the Left derives its political power from the Myth of Oppression, which is for the devoted leftist what the parable of the Fall is for the conservative. Every leftist operates with an historical schema in mind—a passage from slavery to freedom, with the Left as the "chosen people" leading the way to the promised land. That is why the leftist message is as compelling to others as it is to itself. It places its adherents on the side of the victims (an unassailable position in democratic combats) as well as on the side of progress and thus of History itself.
>
> But while the Left connects conservatives with a pseudo-history of domination and oppression, the Right fails to put forward a counter-history that connects Marxist ideas with the political gulags and economic miseries they created. (p. 22)

Yet, the power of Communism to attract is part of its historical apologist's writings, as Ratzinger (2008) reveals:

> The turn that these themes take in Khomyakov is far-reaching. For him, faith is not the power that makes it possible to acknowledge a revealed teaching but, rather, a cognitive power that is higher and more real than merely conceptual thinking. This power of faith, however, according to him, should be attributed, not to the individual, but to the community of the right-believing people. One consequence of this, in his view, is the claim to the absolute subordination of the individual to the collective—in the political realm as well. In his

opinion, the difference between the Western democracies and the right-believing people is "that in a democracy a majority imposes its will on the minority, whereas the right-believing people always decide unanimously, because the individual...always subjects himself interiorly as well to its decisions." The socio-political turn, the fusion of the religious and the socio-political in this concept of "the people", becomes quite clear when Khomyakov views the *mir*, the Russian communist village commune, as the sole truly Christian form of society: "For you the community is the highest manifestation of humanity. In the perfect society the individual must be extinguished." Absolute value of the human being—yes, when he renounces his individual personality and subjects himself completely to the whole. This renunciation...is the principle of a truly free human community and concord, which is consecrated and sanctified by the presence of the Holy Spirit." (p. 33)

In essence then, the later domination of the Russian Orthodox Church by the Communist Party's security force, the KGB, was congruent with some central streams of the history of Russian philosophy and socio-political thought.

The power of Communism to attract and hold the allegiance of the Russian people for as long as it did is also connected to its masquerading as religion, as Marx intended, noted by De Marco & Wiker (2004):

> Marx took the notion of *Original Sin, personal sin,* and *redemption* and purged them of what he believed to be their negative and unattractive associations. Since, for Marx, God did not exist, original Sin could not be a transgression against him. Instead of freeing us from Original Sin, the messianic Marx proclaimed the necessity of the freedom of the proletariat from being exploited by the ruling class. By absorbing individual persons

into *classes*, he absolved them of any capacity for sin as well as any grounds for guilt. Further, since each person is a material product of his class, no conversion is possible. There could be no personal redemption, only a violent revolution that would purge humanity of the capitalist exploiting class. Finally, he relocated paradise to make it an earthly kingdom. He was a messiah for his time who was bringing his people a new religion that was free of personal sin, guilt, the need for penance and suffering, and a Divine Redeemer. He was preaching religion without worship, paradise without God. In other words, he was preaching a parody of religion, offering the husk without the nourishing fruit. And this is why his program could not succeed, even though it could attract. (Italics in original, p. 120)

Gray (2013) writes of that "violent revolution", which became essentially, a genocide:

> One of the features that distinguished Bolshevism from Tsarism was the insistence of Lenin and his followers on the need for a complete overhaul of society. Old-fashioned despots may modernize in piecemeal fashion if doing so seems necessary to maintain their power, but they do not aim at remaking society on a new model, still less at fashioning a new type of humanity. Communist regimes engaged in mass killing in order to achieve these transformations, and paradoxically it is this essentially totalitarian ambition that has appealed to liberals. Here as elsewhere, the commonplace distinction between utopianism and meliorism is less than fundamental. In its predominant forms, liberalism has been in recent times a version of the religion of humanity, and with rare exceptions – Russell is one of the few that come to mind – liberals have seen the Communist experiment as a hyperbolic expression of their own project of

improvement; if the experiment failed, its casualties were incurred for the sake of a progressive cause. To think otherwise – to admit the possibility that the millions who were judged to be less than fully human suffered and died for nothing – would be to question the idea that history is a story of continuing human advance, which for liberals today is an article of faith. That is why, despite all evidence to the contrary, so many of them continue to deny Communism's clear affinities with Fascism. Blindness to the true nature of Communism is an inability to accept that radical evil can come from the pursuit of progress. (n.p.)

There were "affinities with Fascism" as De Marco & Wiker (2004) note:

> By absorbing the person into a *class*, Marx was doing something that parallels Hitler, who absorbed the person into a *race*. Marxism and Nazism had similarly dire outcomes, one leading to Auschwitz, the other to the Gulag Archipelago. They offered mere *existence* without *life*, which, as history has shown, is a precise formula for *death*. (Italics in original, pp. 127-128)

In relation to all that we have examined in this book, the traditional position of the Church regarding Communism, Fatima and the call for the consecration of Russia and the failure to answer that call, what does all of it mean in relation to criminal reformation?

The answer may be a response to the signs of the times, when through the emancipation of class, slaves, women and youth, so painfully and vividly represented by the French Revolution, the American Civil War, the women's suffragette movement, and the 1960's movement of youth, the denouncement of things carried little weight from authority—Question Authority being a clarion call of all emancipation movements—and softer appeals to reason and self-interest were seen as the path to conversion.

As Ratzinger (1987) wrote, describing the evolving process of ecumenism since Vatican II:

> In our discussion of the ideal of collegiality we finally mentioned the catchphrase for which you have surely been waiting: Church as the People of God. But what does it involve? Again, in order to understand it, we must go back to the developments that preceded the Council. After the initial enthusiasm of discovering the idea of the Body of Christ, more profound interpretations and corrections gradually followed along two lines. We have already looked at the first correction; it is found especially in the studies by Henri de Lubac, who developed the concept of the Body of Christ in more concrete terms that led to Eucharistic ecclesiology and, thus, opened it up to the practical questions of the Church's juridical order and of interdependence of local Church and universal Church. The other type of correction began in the late 1930s in Germany, when various theologians observed critically that, with the idea of the Mystical Body, the relation between the visible and the invisible, between law and grace, between order and life ultimately remained unclear. Therefore they suggested the concept "People of God", which is found especially in the Old Testament, as a more easily conveyed description of Church, which incidentally can be more easily conveyed in sociological and juridical terms, whereas the Body of Christ remains an image that is important but, they said, does not satisfy the theological demand for conceptual development.
>
> This initially rather superficial critique of the "Body of Christ" idea was then rounded out from various aspects, which produced the positive content with

which the "People of God" concept entered into the conciliar ecclesiology. The first important point was the controversy about Church membership that arose in connection with the encyclical on the Mystical Body of Christ that Pope Pius XII promulgated on June 29, 1943. At that time he stated that membership in the Church is dependent on three conditions: baptism, right faith, and belonging to the juridical unity of the Church. But with this definition, non-Catholics were entirely excluded from membership in the Church. In a country like Germany in which the ecumenical question is so immediately urgent, this statement necessarily led to vehement debates, especially since the CIC opened up a different perspective. According to the canonical tradition of the Church recorded therein, baptism is the basis for an irrevocable form of constitutive affiliation with the Church. So it became clear that juridical thinking, in certain circumstances, can afford more mobility and openness than a "mystical" understanding. Some wondered whether the image of the Mystical Body was not too narrow as a point of departure to define the manifold forms of affiliation with the Church that have actually existed in the confusion of human history. The image of the Body provides only one notion of affiliation, that of the "member"; someone is a member, or else he is not, and there are no intermediate degrees? So they hit on the expression "People of God", which in this respect is roomier and more flexible. The Constitution on the Church adopted if for this very purpose when it described the situation of non-Catholic Christians by saying that they are somehow "joined" to the Catholic Church and that of non-Christians by saying that they are "related" to the Catholic Church; in both instances, the document relies on the idea of the People of God. (# 15 and 16)

Criminals will respond to truth weightier than the criminal/carceral truth they live by when it is lived by its proponents'. Talk is cheap, but when men and women walk their talk, it is priceless.

Though it is difficult to find within the modern Catholic Church in America those men and women, they do exist, and the golden rod of faith they represent and carry forth, whether it is through their membership and leadership of Church organizations and orders, they are men and women who live by the ancient faith, the faith of our fathers as represented within the Universal Catechisms of Trent and Vatican II, and the papal magisterium, and through them and through all of the faithful, the Holy Catholic Church Christ promised would not fall under the gates of hell, still and will always, stand.

For it is a Church outliving bad popes, bad bishops, bad priests, bad nuns, and keeping within the heart of faith, those innocent faithful who the great apparitions of Our Lady reveal as truly the heart of the Church, as her son proclaimed through Mary Magdalene and Dismas, those who the world does not see, are so often those Christ sees most clearly and holds most closely.

An ambiguous Vatican II, the machinations of Freemasons, Communists—Catholic or non-Catholic—and other secular enemies are but wind in the willows to the infinite roar of Almighty God, creator and king of the world the prince of the world may not influence; and it is the heel of the Virgin Woman who crushes the serpent head of all these worldly troubles whose only effect on the Holy Catholic Church who cannot fall though the Gates of Hell be opened upon her, as they have been since the beginning.

I read laments outlining the end of civilization because the Church has lost her way, misguided by confused popes, corrupt priests, bishops, and nuns yet I do not tremble for the Church and I pray the writers of laments seek greater understanding.

The Church is not a single pope, bishop, priest or nun. The Church is Christ, Mary and the Communion of Saints; and those pilgrims fulfilling their earthly mission will stumble but Christianity will not, for as Hildebrand (1967) writes:

> That the Church summons men to conversion and exhorts them to strive for holiness is in itself a unique actualization of the Kingdom of Christ. The fact that human beings are humbly confessing their sins and that the word of God is being proclaimed *opportune, importune* is a unique triumph of the spirit of Christ. The very existence of the uninterrupted apostolic succession of the papacy and of the many religious orders testifies to the incontestable victory of Christ over the world. And in view of the host of saints in the two thousand years of Christianity, each of whom represents an irruption of the supernatural into this world, who could deny that the words on the obelisk before St. Peter's Basilica have achieved full reality: *Christus vincit, Christus regnat, Christus imperat* (Christ conquers, Christ reigns, Christ rules)? (Italics in original. p. 227)

Indeed, the true Church is the Church beneath the church as, Estes (2004) writes:

> When we walked to church with my grandmother and were in view of the church, she would often say, "See that church?" "Yes, we see that church," we would say. "That's not our church," she would say. "Yes it is, grandma, that's our church." "No, no. Our Church is beneath that church. We don't belong to that brick church. We belong to the Church underneath that church."

> This has stayed with me all my life. When people ask, "How can you still be a Catholic?" I think about the Church beneath the church, and Who lives there, that Heart of Christ that beats and throbs in the underground Church, regardless of the mayhem above it. You can hear that Heart if you lie on the earth. You can hear it at night in your dreams, in prayer, in song, in art...it throbs with endless and immaculate Love. I can feel it in "the Church beneath the church," though I often cannot feel it in the church above ground. The underground Church is the place I return to, over and over again. Health of the Soul. True Refuge of Spirit.

The Vatican II Ecumenical Council of the Church from October 11, 1962 to December 8, 1965 was a significant event in the life of the Church, where all the bishops of the world gathered and under the leadership of the Pope—Pope John XXIII who opened it and Pope Paul VI who closed it—created magisterial documents that still cause controversy through misinterpretation and misrepresentation.

What happened during Vatican II was a struggle between liberal Catholics and conservative Catholics—though inaccurate terms as all Catholics, by their oath of baptism, have to conserve the deposit of faith—but still descriptive and useful. It was a struggle between those who wanted to liberalize her practice and language—often with very good reason—and those who wanted to conserve her practice and language, also, with very good reason.

The liberals largely won, so well documented in two magisterial works: *The Rhine Flows into the Tiber: A History of Vatican II,* by Fr. Ralph M. Wiltgen, S.V.D. (1985) Tan Books, and *Iota Unum: A Study of Changes in the Catholic Church in the XXth Century*, by Romano Amerio (1996) Sarto House.

However, the bottom line of Vatican II is as Hildebrand (1967) wrote:

> When one reads the luminous encyclical *Ecclesiam Suam* of Pope Paul VI or the magnificent "Dogmatic Constitution on the Church" of the Fathers of the council, one cannot but realize the greatness of the Second Vatican Council.
>
> But when one turns to so many contemporary writings—some by very famous theologians, some by minor ones, some by laymen offering us their dilettante theological concoctions—one can only be deeply saddened and even filled with grave apprehension. For it would be difficult to conceive a greater contrast than that between the official documents of Vatican II and the superficial, insipid pronouncements of various theologians and laymen that have broken out everywhere like an infectious disease.
>
> On the one side, we find the true spirit of Christ, the authentic voice of the Church; we find texts that in both form and content breathe a glorious supernatural atmosphere. On the other side, we find a depressing secularization, a complete loss of the *sensus supranaturalis*, a morass of confusion.
>
> The distortion of the authentic nature of the Council produced by this epidemic of theological dilettantism expresses itself chiefly in the false alternatives between which we are all commanded to choose: either to accept the secularization of Christianity or to deny the authority of the Council. (Italics in original. pp. 9-10)

Reading the Vatican II documents again, confirms to me Hildebrand's position is the correct one, and while we may find what we wish in the often dense prose, we can lose ourselves in the interpretations by others, though seeking out the relatively balanced work commenting on Vatican II, such as the aforementioned works by Wiltgen and Amerio, will pay dividends.

The decades-long discussion, or perhaps more accurately described, war, between the liberal wing of the Catholic Church and the conservatives over the interpretation, and in some cases, validity, of its doctrinal and pastoral documents, is an issue that anyone involved in ministry to criminals—inside prison or out—has to come to terms with.

I first became aware of this during the Rite of Christian Initiation for Adults (RCIA) process I was going through in preparation for baptism, but it was not an issue I deeply engaged with until about eight years later.

From the liberal perspective, Vatican II and the Pope who opened it, Pope John XXIII—who many liberals refer to as "Good Pope John", also opened the Church to the modern world with love, compassion, and good humor from the oft perceived closed, rigid, and overly medieval and intellectual Catholic world represented by the Pius Popes, most notably Pope Saint Pius X and Pope Pius XII, though it was also a Church of clarity and one whose writings I will often return to, with those of Pope Pius XII remaining a favorite.

From a conservative perspective—one I largely share—the Pius popes were the last great and strongly traditional leaders of the Catholic world in relation to Communism.

Wiltgen (1985) writes about how Vatican II approached Communism:

On December 3, 1963, the day before the second session ended, Archbishop Geraldo Sigaud of Diamantina, Brazil, personally presented to Cardinal Cicognani petitions addressed to Pope Paul and signed by more than 200 Council Fathers from forty-six countries. These called for a special schema in which "the Catholic social doctrine would be set forth with great clarity, and the errors of Marxism, socialism, and communism would be refuted on philosophical, sociological and economic grounds.

There was no reply from the Pope, but eight months later, on August 6, 1964, he published his first encyclical, *Ecclesiam suam*. In it he called for dialogue with atheistic communism, even though—as he said—there were reasons enough which compelled him, his predecessors and everyone with religious values at heart, "to condemn the ideological systems which deny God and oppress the Church, systems which are often identified with economic, social and political regimes."

The German-speaking and Scandinavian bishops immediately reacted to the encyclical, declaring in their official remarks on the Church in the modern world schema, that it was "probably desirable" to have a "more distinct treatment in the schema of the problem of atheism, and of dialogue with it."

On October 21, 1964, during the third session, the section of the schema dealing with atheism—it carefully avoided the word communism—came up for discussion. Cardinal Suenens, after stating that it did not give lengthy enough treatment to the modern phenomena of militant atheism in its various forms, called for an investigation on why so many men deny God and attack the truth.

Archbishop Paul Yu Pin of Nanking, China, speaking two days later in the name of 70 Council Fathers, asked for the addition of a new chapter on atheistic communism. The Council must not neglect to discuss it, he said, "because communism is one of the greatest, most evident and most unfortunate of modern phenomena." It had to be treated in order to satisfy the expectations of all peoples, "especially those who groan under the yoke of communism and are forced to endure indescribable sorrows unjustly."

Josef Cardinal Beran, exiled archbishop of Prague, residing in Rome, received a Czechoslovakian newspaper clipping which boasted that communists had succeed in infiltrating every commission at the Vatican Council. (pp. 272-273)

The Pastoral Constitution on the Church in the Modern World, *Gaudium et Spes,* does not have a section on Communism, but it examined economic theory, as Charles (1982) notes:

> The capitalist economic theory, with the economic organisation based on it, which has done so much to form the world we live in, was the economic counterpart of a philosophical and political liberalism of which the basic assumption was belief in the absolute autonomy of the individual. It assumed that individual men of property, left free to seek their own interests, would act so as to secure justice and prosperity for all. Such an assumption knew nothing of the warnings of the Gospel about the corrupting powers of wealth. The Council however, in introducing its

observations on economic life reminds us of these injunctions. The fundamental assumptions of liberal capitalism then are not compatible with the Christian ethic. Capitalism is above all materialistic. It has made the ideal of life the pursuit of ever increasing material progress and wealth. The Christian vision, by contrast, is of enjoying God's creation here and his bounty, but doing so with the awareness that here we have no abiding city...

Given this antipathy between economic liberalism or capitalism and the Christian ethic, we cannot assume that since the Church defends the right to own private property, and capitalism embodies the right, the Church therefore defends, still less is responsible for capitalism. Her concept of the social responsibility of private ownership, which is compatible with her insistence that the state has the right to own and run some sections of the economy, demands the very safeguards which were absent from capitalism in its heyday, an absence which led to the injustices it created.

The tremendous power for wealth creation implicit in the application of machines to the production of goods for mass markets (the industrial revolution) was released by men who assumed that unlimited freedom for them would serve all. It did not. The workers on the land and in industry, though they shared an increase in the material standard of living too often did not get a *just* share, while the quality of life—the condition in which they lived and worked, the opportunities open to them for cultural and moral improvement—by no means reflected the part they played in increasing the wealth of nations. That the reaction against the evils of the time should take the form of socialist extremism, summed up in the works of Marx and Engels, is not, therefore, surprising. However, Marx/Engels/Leninism has in practice been shown to be as hard, if not a harder taskmaster, than raw capitalism. Some apologists for Marxism claim that it has never been given a fair trial. But the excesses of Stalinist Russia, or of a Pol Pot's Cambodia, are directly traceable to the faulty ethics of Marx himself. A creed which makes history a sovereign more absolute than any royal absolutism of the past and concedes to those who interpret it a power more complete than any laissez-faire capitalist claimed over his workers is responsible for all the evils that those who appeal to its logic and authority commit. (Italics in original. pp. 375-376)

Drilling down a bit more on Russian Communism, Charles continues:

> Marxist socialism, by contrast, works on the assumption that the wisdom of the central planner is the best determinant of economic activity. On the Russian model, under the Politbureau, the supreme political organisation in the state, the various descending orders of the hierarchy, determine what is to be produced, who is to produce it and how it is to be distributed...
>
> Soviet-type economies are less easily reconcilable with the Catholic social ethic precisely because of their limitations on freedom...
>
> The importance of private property, however, is central to the Church's social teaching and, all things also being equal, she recommends a system in which economic freedom exists. The right to such ownership (including that in productive goods—in modern terms e.g. factories, plant, financial resources for investment) is defended by

> the Scriptures and the Fathers and Doctors of the Church—though if by free choice all could accept goods in common, this is seen to be the higher ideal. However, in the real world it is accepted that private property is necessary for the proper ordering of society and as such it is defended and urged as a good thing in itself. However, such private property must operate for the good of all. It is not an absolute right in either ownership or use; it is subject to social control for the good of all. (*Ibid.* p. 377)

With all of the good things that occurred at Vatican II and also with many of the other unfortunate events that occurred during the Council, the conclusion I have reached—in harmony with the Church—is that Vatican II was a legitimate Ecumenical Council, as traditionally defined by the Church, as Wilhelm (1908) explains:

> Ecumenical Councils are those to which the bishops, and others entitled to vote, are convoked from the whole world under the presidency of the pope or his legates, and the decrees of which, having received papal confirmation, bind all Christians. (n.p.)

It is true many of the documents greatly favored the positions taken by liberals and some even protected Communism, but that was because liberals were much better organized during the Council to ensure their perspective took precedence; but, in many cases—Mass in the vernacular being one—were appropriate decisions.

In the Western world, including Latin America, where Catholicism was well established, opening up the Mass to the vernacular was seen by many as a loss. In the mission fields, such as Africa, it was seen as a blessing.

The Dogmatic Constitution, *Lumen Gentium*, Section 8, saying: "...although many elements of sanctification and of truth are found outside of its visible structure. These elements, as gifts belonging to the Church of Christ, are forces impelling toward catholic unity", implied to many that the Church was not the sole path to salvation as stated by Catholic tradition.

But, while the first sentence seems to say that, the second reaffirms that the full truth is only generated from within the Catholic Church, though it may find its way to other places, as through—for instance—the Protestants via their founder, the Catholic priest, Martin Luther.

This quality of the writings coming from Vatican II, stating one thing but perhaps implying another, is, I have come to realize, one of the methods the Church has decided upon for confronting modernity—maintaining the clarity of tradition while allowing the ambiguity of the times.

This method softens the clarity of the Church's one truth and allows those who would run from that sort of 'golden rod clarity' to stick around.

It is not a method I particularly like, but I certainly see the wisdom of it, and it may lay at the heart of the Church's softening of its relations with Communism, especially through the long papacy of John Paul II, the first pope from a Communist Country, who had several decades of dealing with the Communists while priest, bishop, and cardinal in Poland; and may have decided that, once pope, that there could be a more effective way of converting Communists than the historical method developed by previous popes.

And the results may very well be seen in the recent speculation that the Orthodox Church is very close to rejoining the Roman Catholic fold, as reported by Fraser & Warren (March 18, 2013):

> ANKARA, Turkey (AP) — Bartholomew I, the spiritual leader of the world's Orthodox Christians, will attend Pope Francis' installation Mass — the first time a patriarch from the Istanbul-based church has attended a papal investiture since the two branches of Christianity split nearly 1,000 years ago.
>
> Bartholomew said he is doing that to underscore the importance of "friendly ties" between the churches and expectations that the new pontiff will advance rapprochement efforts that began decades ago.
>
> It's a sentiment that many leaders of other faiths are expressing ahead of Tuesday's installation, which is drawing dozens of Jewish, Orthodox and other Christian leaders to Rome for the start of a pontificate that is poised to deepen the Vatican's ecumenical and interfaith efforts given Francis' namesake and own history.
>
> Those who knew Jorge Mario Bergoglio as leader of Argentina's Catholic Church say promoting interfaith dialogue was at the heart of his view of the what the Catholic faith should be about — an outward-reaching, bottom-up effort to improve lives, no matter what people's faith.
>
> "He's the one who opened the cathedral of Buenos Aires for interfaith ceremonies, like when we prayed for peace. He's not one of those who waits for you to call them to participate in these events — he promotes them," Buenos Aires Rabbi Alejandro Avruj told The Associated Press on Monday. (n.p.)

This being said, it is still troubling that the Church promised to not speak of Communism during Vatican II, especially considering the perspective on that silence mentioned by Amerio (1996):

> The weakening of the logical sense, which is characteristic of the spirit of the age, has taken from the Church too its repugnance to mutually contradictory assertions. The opening speech of the council lauds the freedom of the contemporary Church at a time when, as the speech itself recognizes, many bishops are in prison for their faithfulness to Christ and when, thanks to an agreement sought by the Pope the council finds itself bound by a commitment not to condemn communism. This contradiction, although important, remains nonetheless secondary in comparison to that fundamental contradiction by which the renewal of the Church is based on an opening to the world, while the most important, essential and decisive of the world's problems, namely communism, is left out of account. (p. 77)

This is very troubling and little seems resolved about the trouble by characterizing thinking and speaking about totalitarianism without reference to the very model of totalitarianism since 1917, Communism.

We see in the writings of many superb thinkers, even some who wrote against the Church, such as Ayn Rand, the essentials of truth, once we have gotten hold of the whole truth from which to view them; but sadly, many of these thinkers ended their lives in bitterness, sadness, acrimony, and ultimately failure as deep as the chasm between their discovered truth and the full truth they never accepted.

One aspect of Fatima that I've not seen mentioned much is its timeliness. Our Holy Mother promised in 1917 she would call for the consecration of Russia, warning of great suffering if that consecration was not carried out.

The Church says it was carried out within the consecration of the entire world by Pope John Paul II, and Sister Lucia, one of the Fatima children, agreed.

However, it would seem to me, and I certainly have no special knowledge other than my study of the issue for the past couple of years, that when she promised on July 13, 1917 to call for the consecration of Russia and following it up with the specific call within a vision to Sister Lucia on June 13, 1929, she meant it to take place then and when we consider the sufferings of the world since—Communist takeover of Russia and the approximately 100 million estimated that were killed by its edicts, world-wide depression, WWII and the genocide against the Jewish people taking the lives of six million, Communist takeover of China, Korea, and Southeast Asia and the millions of lives lost in the process, and the hundreds of millions lost to abortion, the sexual abuse crisis in the Church—it is hard to see how any one century could have been much worse.

The still active effort to have the pope consecrate Russia, while certainly not really harmful as Russia is a criminal state, the time it should have been done was the time our Holy Mother called for it to be done, and since it was not done, much of the damage surely has already been done.

Our walking the talk of Catholicism, our prayers for the world, for our faith, for the Holy Father, priests and nuns, all religious and all the faithful are still the one certain way we can help Our Lord help our world.

The ambiguity of the Catechism produced by Vatican II cuts both ways; solidifying tradition or disrupting it, depending on who is reading it.

The faithful will hew to the traditional doctrine woven through it, the dissident will see innovation and disruption to traditional doctrine and will hew to that, and so it has always been, even since the Garden.

Vatican II was a true council, congruent with the tradition of many ecumenical councils of the Church in the world, but it also continued the eternal war the Church in the world has been engaged, with more ammunition perhaps given to Satan than to Christ; but regardless of the quantity of ammunition, the ultimate end has already been decided by God and, as written since the Garden, Satan loses.

Ammunition is only as sound as the gun from which it is fired.

Though the ambiguity of Vatican II and the Catechism later promulgated by Pope John Paul II, gave many bullets to Satan in his penetration of the Church, it also identified his minions through their use of those bullets; as did the interpretations of Vatican II and the Catechism as supporting Catholic dogma identify those who stood with Peter, Christ and Mary.

A definition from Hardon (1999) may be helpful here:

> **Pastoral Theology.** The practical application of scientific theology to the care of souls in the sacred ministry. Its purpose is to render this ministry more effective by the use of proven methods of dealing with the spiritual needs of individuals or groups of the faithful. A relatively new discipline, it came into being to cope with the increasingly complex and changing circumstances

of modern life. It draws on the principles and methodology of both the secular and the sacred sciences, with special concern to help the people live out their Christian commitments in conflict with a hostile or at least indifferent non-Christian society. (p. 497)

Scientific theology is clearly that from St. Thomas Aquinas and pastoral theology would describe that which has been coming from the Vatican since Pope John XXIII, but both are a reflection of the traditional theology of the Catholic Church, but expressed in different ways, for different times; a strategy straight from St. Paul.

For John Paul II, knowing from personal experience that Communism does not work and ultimately degrades into corruption and criminality; he knew that salvation would then be possible, conversion would then be possible, for he knew that the 2,000 years of Catholic history enduring truth and practice would attract the ideological riven Communist who had seen his bright vision become a dark nightmare.

Our Church is a pilgrim Church, as Amerio (1996) explains:

> It is appropriate here to formulate the law of the historical conservation of the Church, a law which also constitutes her ultimate apologetic criterion. The Church is founded on the Word Incarnate, that is, on a divinely revealed truth. She is also given sufficient energies to conform her own life to that truth; it is a dogma of faith that virtue is always possible. Nonetheless, the Church is only in danger of perishing if she loses the truth, not if she fails to live up to it. The pilgrim Church is, as it were, simultaneously condemned to imperfection in her activity, and to repentance: in the modern phrase, the Church is in a continual

> state of conversion. She is not destroyed when human weakness conflicts with her own teaching (that contradiction is inherent in the Church's pilgrim condition); but she is destroyed when corruption reaches the level of corroding dogma, and of preaching in theory the corruptions which exist in practice. (Ibid. p. 18)

Our Church is divinely founded and divinely protected though worldly stained, even to the point of harboring satanic evil, a point which Balthasar (1991) captures describing the Church as both whore and virgin:

> When Luther dares to equate the Roman Church with the whore of Babylon, it strikes us as the height of blasphemy. But he was not the first to coin the phrase. Similar things can be found in Wycliffe and Hus, and their language was not a complete innovation but the violent simplification and coarsening of a very old *theologoumenon*. This in turn has its origin in the Old Testament, in the words of judgment spoken by God, the betrayed Husband, against the archwhore Jerusalem, and in the New Testament's application of these texts, which are so fundamental to the Old. Now it is true that the Church regards herself as profoundly different from the unfaithful synagogue; in her there is at least one identifiable place where she is perfectly pure and unchangeably faithful. No believer, no Christian theologian (including Luther), would ever doubt these truths. But is that the only thing she has to be? Could the real *Ekklesia*, made up of *these* particular believers, be something different? Christians of other times have unhesitatingly acknowledged that it would be rash to deny these possibilities a priori. (Italics in original. p. 193)

Our Church—and here we must clearly include Jerusalem of the Old Covenant and stretching back to Genesis—has sometimes whored herself and the condemnations as the Whore of Babylon is therefore accurate, as is the acclamation as Holy Mother Church.

Both Marys—the mother of Jesus and the Magdalene—were present at the close of the Old Covenant and the opening of the New and as Balthasar continues:

> Without endangering the immaculateness, holiness, and infallibility of the Church, one must look the other reality in the eye and not exclude it from consideration. Much would be gained if Christians learned more and more to realize at what price the holiness of the Church has been purchased. (*Ibid.* p. 198)

Now, that the narrative within the minds of most Americans, is that Communism is dead, what is the point mulling it over once again.

The point is, dear reader, that the very same forgetfulness of incarnate evil represented by Communism is a forgetfulness clouding the mind for time immemorial when it comes to the works of those principalities and powers allied with Satan against God and the Church.

It is happening again, now, today, always, regarding the historical implacable enemy of the Church, rampant evil and the tendency of people to ignore it, deny it, hope it leaves them, us, alone.

Communism, perhaps in new forms—while retaining its historical nature in Russia—is certainly not dead, as Douzinas & Zizek (2010) note:

> The long night of the left is drawing to a close. The defeat, denunciations and despair of the 1980s

and 1990s, the triumphalist 'end of history', the unipolar world of American hegemony—all are fast becoming old news....

The return of history has led to a renewed interest in radical ideas and politics. The twenty-first century left can finally leave behind the introspection, contrition and penance that followed the fall of the Soviet Union. The left which aligned itself with 'actually existing socialism' ahs disappeared or turned into a historical curiosity. New forms of radical militancy and mobilization have marked the return to politics. In Latin America, the different new lefts in Bolivia, Venezuela and Brazil are developing unprecedented and imaginative national paths to socialism. In the United States, the election of Barack Obama was a symbolic moment hailed throughout the world as a sign of historical progress. In India, China and Africa, dissent, resistance and rebellion have replaced the somnolent and fearful 1990s (vii-viii)

The more the financial systems of the world struggle to provide fairness and opportunity to their citizens, the more Communism wends its way in through the weakened defenses.

Do we not all fall prey to this and do we not all know the surest defense is a strong relationship with God through prayer and living a life of as much sanctity as we can, remembering that betrayal is written into our very bones and blood, beginning with Adam and Eve.

Afterword

After studying the issue, the conclusion I reached in our annual policy primer of this year for members of the Lampstand Foundation: *Catholicism, Communism & Criminal Reformation*, regarding the failure of the Council to vigorously condemn Communism as had so many previous popes, was that, at best, Vatican II was a council whose decisions on this issue were confused.

My research into the subject has continued as I have worked on this book covering the same ground, and now I am reaching the conclusion that what I saw then as confusion may very well have been wisdom.

I recently came across this from O'Malley (2008):

> No matter where authority in the church is located, in what manner is it to be wielded? That is a third issue-under-the-issues, suggested by the word "charism." Here the council becomes more explicit by introducing a new vocabulary and literary form. Words like "charism," "dialogue," "partnership," "cooperation," and "friendship" indicate a new style for the exercise of authority and implicitly advocate a conversion to a new style of thinking, speaking, and behaving, a change from a more authoritarian and unidirectional style to a more reciprocal and responsive model. This change effected a redefinition of what councils are and what they are supposed to accomplish. Vatican II so radically modified the legislative and judicial model that had prevailed since the first council, Nicaea, in 325, that it virtually abandoned it. It its place Vatican II put a model largely based on persuasion and invitation. This was a momentous shift. (p. 11)

Reminding myself of what the word "charism" means by going to my Hardon (1999), was helpful:

> Charisms: Literally "gifts of grace" (charismata), described by St. Paul as gratuitous blessings of an extraordinary and transitory nature conferred directly for the good of others. Indirectly they may also benefit the one who possesses the charisms. But their immediate purpose is for the spiritual welfare of the Christina community. (p. 94)

One of the great benefits of the ambiguity expressed in the interpretations of the Council's work, was how it has drawn out the venom that had lain festering in the Church as those religious and laity who had simmered in dissent now flamed into a raging fire of opposition and all now know who they are and of whom they speak, as they cast off their religious garb and way of life.

Remembering the world-wide atmosphere of the 1960s in which Vatican II evolved, where we largely moved from the historical age of the tyrants, kings, and dictators to the age of committees and dialogue; is it any wonder that the Vatican, accustomed more than any other institution in the world, to think in terms of centuries rather than years, would play a leading role in this shift, an idea with deepened resonance watching the evolving papacy of our new Holy Father as a congruent link in the Holy Fathers since Vatican II.

When I last got out of prison in August of 1969, and returned to California, I immediately was swept up in the revolutionary movement wherein criminals, paradoxically, were seen as leaders, as Cummins (1994) writes:

> In the Bay Area, for a large percentage of leftists, prison themes at the end of the 1960's gained prominence for a short time, even eclipsing the importance of protests late in the decade against

> the Vietnam War and the broader issue of race, or even the lure of the counterculture themes of sex and drugs. (p.126)

Though my deepest involvement was with the counterculture themes, the mantra that most of us shared during that period was "Question Authority"; and coming out of the 1950s, where the most authoritative institutions of the culture wrapped obedience to authority in steel webs, it was an incredibly liberating—but as we eventually learned, corrosive—mantra, as those of us who lived through that time remember.

At that time, my bibles were *The Wisdom of the Sands* by Antoine de Saint Exupery, which I embraced during my last stretch in prison at McNeil Island Federal Penitentiary, and *The Whole Earth Catalog*, which someone thrust into my hands shortly after I had gotten out and said "Here, catch up." My drug of choice was mescaline, and in that befuddled state, I believed we—the smiley long-haired bearded ones and our earth mother women—were creating a new world, which seemed to be validated in the other beaming faces (who were also peaked out on psychedelics) I encountered as I walked the streets of Lake Tahoe, Berkeley, San Francisco, Vancouver, British Columbia, and all points in between, with my small entourage.

We believed psychedelics opened the doors of perception— as Aldous Huxley so aptly phrased— allowing us to discover our latent powers, and when *The Aquarian Conspiracy* by Marilyn Ferguson was published, we knew that what we had thought we were doing was in fact what we had been about, as Ferguson (1980) writes:

> A leaderless but powerful network is working to bring about radical change in the United States. Its members have broken with certain key elements of Western thought, and they may even have broken continuity with history.

> This network is the Aquarian Conspiracy. It is a conspiracy without a political doctrine. Without a manifesto. With conspirators who seek power only to disperse it, and whose strategies are pragmatic, even scientific, but whose perspective sound so mystical that they hesitate to discuss it. Activists asking different kinds of questions, challenging the establishment from within.
>
> Broader than reform, deeper than revolution, this benign conspiracy for a new human agenda has triggered the most rapid cultural realignment in history. The great shuddering irrevocable shift overtaking us is not a new political, religious, or philosophical system. It is a new mind—the ascendance of a startling worldview that gathers into its framework break-through science and insights from earliest recorded thought. (p. 23)

Later, much later, I would discover that the *real*, powerful network was founded by Christ and led by Peter which had existed for millennia, radically changing the meaning of life on earth.

This was the Catholic Church, the foundation of Western thought; and the saints of the Church had been accessing latent human powers through the grace of God ever since.

Within this environment of change, the decision by Vatican II to focus on change or as the elements were called then: *aggiornamento, development,* and *ressourcement,* or, modernizing, evolving, and returning to sources, respectively, was a wise response to the spirit of the Aquarian times.

One of the ideas, once obscured but now leaping out, is that rather than continuing the strong pronouncements against Communism characterizing the first five decades of the 20th Century, the Church now decided *to embrace in order to convert* Communism, as O'Malley (2008) notes:

> The style of discourse the council adopted was, ...made up of two essential elements, a genre and a vocabulary appropriate to it....
>
> The genre...is what the Roman authors called...the panegyric, and its home is in what is traditionally known as humanistic culture...
>
> Its goal is the winning of internal assent, not the imposition of conformity from the outside...
>
> While it raises appreciation, it creates or fosters among those it addresses a realization that they all share (or should share) the same ideals and need to work together to achieve them. (pp. 46-48)
>
> On March 7 [1963] John [Pope John XXIII] had received in audience Alexis Adzhubei, the editor of Izvestia, the notorious Soviet newspaper, and son-in-law of Nikita Khrushchev, the Soviet chairman. The meeting caused a sensation. On that same day the International Balzan Foundation awarded John its prize in recognition of his work for peace. In his acceptance speech he shocked many who looked upon the church as the leader in the campaign against Communism when he said that "on the plane of international competition, whether armed or merely verbal, [the church maintains] an absolute neutrality." (pp. 165-166)

And one wonders how much this approach opened the door for Pope John Paul II to play one of the leading roles in vanquishing the Soviet empire a few decades later, and to the emerging potential coming together of the Russian Orthodox with Rome.

On the other hand, this may well be the making a bad situation a little better by acknowledging the reality on the ground; the bad situation being the failure of Peter and the bishops to consecrate Russia to the Immaculate Heart of the Holy Mother of God, and the acknowledgement that the Church was not able to defeat Communism during its formative stage through the intersession of the Holy Mother; the best policy now might be to dialogue with them, seeking men and women of good will with whom conversion might be possible; and that might very well be a wise strategy.

The decision to engage rather than condemn Communism might prove to be a wise decision or it might prove to be, as the current pope and the two previously have done by calling for the abolition of capital punishment, indicate a lack of understanding of evil.

While this may seem fanciful for men—the Vicars of Christ on earth—whose life is focused on helping sinners, but an examination of the life of priests can reveal little opportunity to fully appreciate the hardness and clarity of evil intent, of an evil life lived consciously.

Though the three Holy Fathers—one who dealt with the Communists, one with Nazis and one with a military dictatorship—have seen evil, one would think their knowledge would be deep but here is where the within and the without of the human soul crucially determines soul knowledge and why many traditions advocate salvation coming through self-degradation; but not sought as Rimbaud and Rasputin, but having happened in life, like Pope Saint Callistus, the former criminal who became pope, perhaps one of the greatest popes.

Though the situation may be more dire, as Rao (2013) writes:

> The Catholic world has been shaken by the recent interview with Pope Francis appearing in the Jesuit journal, La Civiltà Cattolica [Italian for Catholic Civilization, it is a periodical published since 1850 without interruptions by the Jesuits in Rome...

For La Civiltà Cattolica was founded in 1850 precisely to combat the obvious Church weakness and surrender to willfulness that were the inevitable by-product of the kind of "open" approach to "diverse" modern men that the Holy Father is now once again promoting. Perhaps recalling this life-giving lesson from the journal's past may inspire second thoughts tempering the truly deadening effect of the words found in its current pages...

We, as modern Catholics, forced to live in the world created for us by the abandonment of the lessons learned by La Civiltà Cattolica in the 1850's, are now in almost exactly the same boat that its editors were in the year that they founded that journal—except with bigger leaks in the hull. Despite what the Holy Father says, we, in 2013, have no recollection of the Church's ever having given up that dialogue with the modern world that began anew in the 1960's (an era that I truly wish were dead and buried for good). We have been living with that dialogue for over fifty years now, armed with precepts promoted by the progeny of Lamennais, and we have never ceased to pay the price for it. We are all the victims of Restorationism—the Restoration of the State of Forgetfulness about the entirety of the Catholic Faith that we escaped from in the Nineteenth Century. We have once again successfully forgotten the Tradition we already forgot once before. We have succeeded in voluntarily achieving a Second Childhood whose inevitable ill effects were described for us in detail in the 1850's. We have been handed over, hook, line, and sinker into the hands of the willful, who have been publically exulting that we are longing for still "more of the same". We are, as St. Peter says, like dogs returned to their vomit. (n.p.)

Again, though I am still researching and praying about all of this, it does add to the wonder that this convert feels as I come to learn more and more about my adopted faith, and am validated in my knowledge—especially for those of us approaching the Church intellectually, which is the way most penitential professional criminals will actually convert—that lifelong study is crucial to truly understand and appreciate the Church and her social teaching.

As for Fatima, Mirus (2013) reminds us of the actual standing of private revelations:

> But the second point I wish to make is that even if the Church judges a private revelation as "worthy of belief" and suitable for the devotion of the faithful, she requires nobody to believe it. These things are not matters of Faith. Not even a pope has to believe in them, even though a prior pope may have reached an affirmative judgment. Some avid promoters of Fatima, however, have tried to impose this private revelation on the Church herself, by referring to it as a special category of revelation, as I indicated. But no such category exists in the Church's theological lexicon. It is rather a category invented by some ill-advised proponents of the Fatima message who are disgruntled by what they see as the Church's failure to respond to Fatima as these same proponents would have her do.
>
> Revelation is called "public" if it is entrusted to the Church as the foundation of her mission—that is, if it is part of the deposit of faith which the Church exists to conserve, explain and propagate. This Revelation (capital R) was completed in Jesus Christ, communicated to the apostles, and closed with the death of the last apostle. It and it alone contains everything Our Lord desired us to know for our salvation. The Church can neither ignore nor change it; she is utterly bound by it.

> In contrast, all other revelations (small r, such as audible locutions and visible apparitions and interior communications) are to private persons. These do not bind the Church in any way, nor are they an addition to Revelation, nor do they contain, even if approved, anything necessary for salvation that is not already found in Revelation itself. Because these things add nothing to Revelation (capital R), no one is obliged to believe any private revelation even if the Church, at some point, has made a positive judgment as to its authenticity as a private revelation. The assent of Faith is simply not required. The message may awaken us quite wonderfully, but our response is an inessential matter of human discernment. (n.p.)

Our faith requires us to live in the present, not in an imagined past or dreamt future.

Our Catholic faith requires us to honor her tenets, and to live, supernaturally, in the present, and always remember, our Church is a Church of the Word, not a Church of the human, the Eternal Church underneath the brick church.

With Peter, to Christ, through Mary.

References

Amerio, R. (1996). *Iota unum: A study of changes in the Catholic church in the XXth century.* Kansas City, Missouri: Sarto House.

Applebaum, A. (2012). *Iron curtain: The crushing of Eastern Europe 1944-1956.* New York: Doubleday.

Arendzen, J. (1909). Gnosticism. In *The Catholic Encyclopedia.* New York: Robert Appleton Company. (Retrieved February 12, 2013 from: http://www.newadvent.org/cathen/06592a.htm

Balthasar, H.U.V. (1991). *Spouse of the word: Explorations in theology* (Vols. 1-4). San Francisco: Ignatius Press.

Belloc, H. (1938). *The great heresies.* (1991 ed.) Rockford, Illinois: Tan Books and Publishers, Inc.

Berdyaev, N. (1960). *The origin of Russian communism.* United States of America: The University of Michigan Press.

Berdyaev, N. (1977). Philosophical truth and the moral truth of the intelligentsia. In Shragin, B. & Todd, A. (Eds.). *Landmarks: A collection of essays on the Russian intelligentsia.* (pp. 3-22) New York: Karz Howard.

Berdyaev, N. (2006). *The meaning of history.* New Brunswick: Transaction publishers.

Bowman, J. (2006). *Honor: A history.* New York: Encounter Books.

Brown, L. (ed.) (1993). *The new shorter Oxford English*

dictionary. (Vols. 1-2). Oxford: Clarendon Press.

Byrne, C. (2010). *The Catholic worker movement (1933-1980): A critical analysis.* United Kingdom: AuthorHouse UK Ltd.

Carnegie, A. (1998). [1889]. *The gospel of wealth.* Bedford, Massachusetts: Applewood Books.

Carson, E. A. & Sabol, W. J. (December 2012) *Prisoners in 2011*, U.S. Department of Justice, Office of Justice Programs, Bureau of Criminal Statistics. (pp. 9-10) Retrieved March 22, 2013 from: http://bjs.gov/content/pub/pdf/p11.pdf

Catholic News Agency. (August 14, 2013). Pope Francis to Consecrate the World to Mary's Immaculate Heart, *National Catholic Register.* Retrieved August 16, 2013 from: http://www.ncregister.com/daily-news/pope-francis-to-consecrate-the-world-to-marys-immaculate-heart

Chambers, W. (1952). (50th Anniversary Edition). *Witness.* Washington, D.C.: Regnery Publishing, Inc.

Collier, P. & Horowitz. D. (1996). *It's a war stupid.* Los Angeles, California: Center for the Study of Popular Culture. Retrieved November 30, 2012 from: http://www.discoverthenetworks.org/Articles/Itsa WarStupid.pdf

Congregation for the Doctrine of the Faith. (1986). *Instruction on Christian freedom and liberation,* March 22, 1986, Retrieved June 2, 2012 from: http://www.vatican.ca/roman_curia/congrgations /cfaith/documents/rc_con/cfaith_doc_19860322_ freedom-liberation_en.html

Coulter, A. (2003). *Treason: Liberal treachery from the*

cold war to the war on terrorism. New York: Crown Forum.

Courtois, S., Werth, N., Panne, J.L., Paczkowski, A., Bartosek, K. & Margolin, J.L. (1999). *The black book of Communism: Crimes, terror, repression*. Cambridge, Massachusetts; Harvard University Press.

Cort, J. C. (2003). *Dreadful conversions: The making of a Catholic socialist*. New York: Fordham University Press.

Cummins, E. (1994). *The rise and fall of California's radical prison movement*. Stanford, California: Stanford University Press.

De Marco, D. & Wiker, B.D. (2004). *Architects of the culture of death*. San Francisco: Ignatius Press.

Douzinas, C. & Zizek, S. (Eds.) (2010). Introduction. *The idea of communism*. New York: Verso.

Estes, C. P. (2004). The church beneath the church, *Closing address to the 2004 CTA National Conference*

Fanon, F. (1966). *The wretched of the earth*. (C. Farrington, Trans.) New York: Grove Press Inc.

Ferguson, M. (1980). *The Aquarian conspiracy: Personal and social transformation in the 1980s*. Los Angeles: J. P. Tarcher, Inc.

Fraser, S. & Warren, M. (March 18, 2013). Orthodox patriarch to Rome for pope's installation. *Associated Press*. Retrieved March 28, 2013 from: http://news.yahoo.com/orthodox-patriarch-rome-popes-installation-111214963.html

Friedman, L. J. & McGarvey, M. D. (Eds.). (2003). *Charity, philanthropy, and civility in American history.* Cambridge, United Kingdom: Cambridge University Press.

Garcia, A. F. (2009, July 7) *Color Variations in Communism - Part I.* Retrieved November 12, 2012 from: http://www.traditioninaction.org/HotTopics/j027ht_ColorChange_Garcia.html

Goldberg, M. (2013, October 14). A Generation of Intellectuals Shaped by 2008 Crash Rescues Marx From History's Dustbin, *Tablet.* Retrieved October 14, 2013 from http://www.tabletmag.com/jewish-news-and-politics/148162/young-intellectuals-find-marx?all=1

Gray, J. (2013, January 2) Communism, Facism, and liberals now. *The Times Literary Supplement.* Retrieved January 19, 2013 from http://www.the-tls.co.uk/tls/public/article1186584.ece

Gutierrez, G. (1988). *A theology of liberation: History, politics, and salvation.* Maryknoll, New York: Orbis Books.

Hardon. J. A. (1999). *Modern Catholic dictionary.* Bardstown, Kentucky: Eternal Life.

Hildebrand, D. V. (1967). *Trojan horse in the city of God: The Catholic crisis explained.* Manchester, New Hampshire: Sophia Institute Press.

Johnson, P. (1991). *Modern times: The world from the Twenties to the Nineties.* (Revised ed.) New York: HarperCollins Publishers.

Johnston, F. (1980). *Fatima: The great sign.* Rockford, Illinois: Tan Books and Publishers, Inc.

Kaufmann, W. (1975). *Existentialism from Dostoevsky to Sartre.* (Revised Ed.). New York: Penguin Group.

Kengor, P. (2010). *Dupes: How America's adversaries have manipulated progressives for a century.* Wilmington, Delaware: Intercollegiate Studies Institute, ISI Books.

Kishkovsky, S. (2013, July 28). Putin in Ukraine to Celebrate a Christian Anniversary. *New York Times. Western Edition.*

Koestler, A. (2001). *The initiates: Arthur Koestler.* (In Crossman, R. H. Ed.). *The god that failed.* (pp. 15-75) New York: Columbia University Press.

Kramer, P. Fr. (2010). *The Devil's final battle: How rejection of the Fatima prophecies imminently threatens the Church and the World.* (2nd Ed.) The Missionary Association: Terryville, Connecticut.

Laqueur, W. (1994). *The dream that failed: Reflections on the Soviet Union.* New York: Oxford University Press.

Lewy, G. (1988). *Peace & revolution: The moral crisis of American pacifism.* Grand Rapids, Michigan: William B. Eerdmans Publishing Company.

Lucas, E. (2012). *Deception: The untold story of east-west espionage today.* New York: Walker & Company.

Lukenbill, D. (2012). *The criminal's search for God: Sources.* Sacramento, California: The Lampstand Foundation.

Martin, J. (2013, April) An epic in search of an ending. *New Oxford Review. LXXX*(3), 22-27.

Martin, M. (1987). *The Jesuits, the society of Jesus and the betrayal of the Roman Catholic church.* New York: Linden Press, Simon and Schuster.

Marx. K. & Engels, F. (9198). *The communist manifesto: A modern edition.* (S. Moore, Trans., English Edition, 1888). New York: Verso. (Original work published in 1848)

McGregor, R. (2010). *The party: The secret world of China's communist rulers.* New York: HarperCollins Publishers.

McDonough, P. & Bianchi, E. C. (2002). *Passionate uncertainty: Inside the American Jesuits.* Berkeley: University of California Press.

Miller, W. D. (1973). *A harsh and dreadful love: Dorothy Day and the Catholic worker movement.* New York: Liveright.

Mirus, J. (2013, October 17). The Consecration and Fatima, Redux, *Catholic Culture.* Retrieved October 18, 2013 from http://www.catholicculture.org/commentary/otc.cfm?id=1120

Mises, L. V. (1981). *Socialism: An economic and sociological analysis.* (Kahane, J. Trans.). Indianapolis: Liberty Fund.

Moynihan, M.C. (2013, February). Red Spread: Book Review on *Iron Curtain: The Crushing of Eastern Europe, 1944-1956. Commentary Magazine,* Retrieved February 3, 2013 from: http://www.commentarymagazine.com/articles/red-spread/

Murphy, D. S., Richards, S. C. & Fuleihan, B. (2012). Policy options to mitigate the criminal record barrier to employment. *Journal of Prisoners on Prisons, 21*(1 & 2), 90-104.

Murray, J. C. (1960). *We hold these truths: Catholic reflections on the American proposition.* New York: Sheed and Ward.

Nietzsche, F. W. (1959). *The portable Nietzsche.* (Kaufmann, W., Ed.) New York: Penguin Books.

Olasky, M. (1992). *The tragedy of American compassion.* Washington, D. C.: Regnery Publishing, Inc.

O'Malley, J. W. (2008). *What happened at Vatican II.* Cambridge, Massachusetts: The Belknap Press of Harvard University Press.

Pacepa, I. M. & Rychlak, R. J. (2013). *Disinformation: Former spy chief reveals secret strategies for undermining freedom, attacking religion, and promoting terrorism.* Washington D.C.: WND Books.

Pentin, E. (2013, July 25). *Bringing the Liturgy Back to the Real Vatican II*, Retrieved July 26, 2013 from http://www.zenit.org/en/articles/bringing-the-liturgy-back-to-the-real-vatican-ii

Pope Leo XIII, (1878) *Quod Apostolici Muneris.* Retrieved May 21, 2012 from: http://www.vatican.va/holy_father/leo_xiii/encyclicals/documents/hf_l-xiii_enc_28121878_quod-apostolici-muneris_en.html

Pope Pius XI. (1937, March 19). *Divini redemptoras: Encyclical of Pope Pius XI on atheistic Communism.* Retrieved July 10, 2012 from: http://www.vatican.va.holy_father/pius_xi/encycli

cals/documents/hf_p-xi_enc_19031937_divini-redemptoris_en.html

Rand, A. (1966). *Capitalism: The unknown ideal.* New York: The New American Library.

Rao, J. (2013). Dialogue with the Living Dead, A Deadening Moment in the Civiltà's Present Critiqued by its Living Past. *Remnant Newspaper*, Retrieved October 3, 2013 from: http://remnantnewspaper.com/Archives/2013-0930-rao-civilta-cattholica-pope-francis.htm

Ratzinger, J.C. (1987). *Church, ecumenism, and politics*: *New endeavors in ecclesiology.* San Francisco: Ignatius Press.

Ratzinger, J. C. (1996). *Called to communion: Understanding the Church today.* San Francisco: Ignatius Press.

Ratzinger, J. C. (2008). *Church, ecumenism, and politics: New endeavors in ecclesiology.* (Miller, M.J. et al., Trans.) San Francisco: Ignatius Press.

Reed, J. (1935). *Ten days that shook the world.* New York: The Modern Library.

Charles, R. & Maclaren, D. (1982). *The social teachings of Vatican II: Its origin and development.* San Francisco: Ignatius Press.

Romerstein, H. & Breindel, E. (2000). *The Venona secrets: Exposing Soviet espionage and America's traitors.* Washington, D.C.: Regnery Publishing, Inc.

Rose, D. C. (2013, April 1) Social justice theory: A solution in search of a problem. *Library of Law & Liberty.* Retrieved April 8, 2013 from: http://www.libertylawsite.org/liberty-forum/social-justice-theory-a-solution-in-search-of-a-problem/

Sartre, J. P. (1963). *Saint Genet: Actor and martyr.* (B. Frechtman, Trans.). New York: George Braziller, Inc.

Satter, D. (2003). *Darkness at dawn: The rise of the Russian criminal state.* New Haven & London: Yale University Press.

Satter, D. (2012). *It was a long time ago, and it never happened anyway: Russia and the Communist past.* New Haven & London: Yale University Press.

Sheen, F. J. (1948). *Communism and the conscience of the West.* New York: Bobbs-Merrill Company

Sciabarra, C. M. (1995). *Ayn Rand: The Russian radical.* University Park, Pennsylvania: The Pennsylvania State University Press.

Sheed, F. J. (1946). *Theology and sanity.* New York: Sheed & Ward.

Solzhenitsyn, A. (1976). *Warning to the west.* New York: Farrar, Strauss and Giroux.

Sowell, T. (2013, July 5) The Left's Central Delusion, *National Review Online* . Retrieved July 27, 2013 from: http://www.nationalreview.com/article/352704/lefts-central-delusion-thomas-sowell

Sterling, C. (1994). *Thieves' world: The threat of the new global network of organized crime.* New York: Simon & Schuster.

Storck, T. What is Thomism & why does it matter: Why study philosophy? *New Oxford Review. LXXX.* 22-26.

Szamuely, T. (1974). *The Russian tradition*. (R. Conquest, Ed.). London: Secker & Warburg.

U.S. Catholic Interview. (March 2010). *U.S. Catholic Magazine.* Retrieved March 25, 2013 from: http://www.uscatholic.org/culture/social-justice/2010/01/do-you-hear-cry-poor-liberation-theology-today

Walsh, E, A. (S.J.) (1928). *The fall of the Russian empire: The story of the last of the Romanovs and the coming of the Bolsheviks.* Fort Collins: Roman Catholic Books.

Weigel, G. (1987). *Tranquillitas ordinis: The present failure and future promise of American Catholic thought on war and peace.* New York: Oxford University Press.

Weigel, G. (2010). *The end and the beginning: Pope John Paul II—The victory of freedom, the last years, the legacy.* New York: Doubleday.

Weigel, G. (2012, August 14). *Can Organ-harvesters Be Number One?* Ethics & Public Policy Center. Retrieved August 14, 2012 from: http://www.eppc.org/publications/pubID.4822/pub_detail.asp

West, D. (2013). *American betrayal: The secret assault on our nation's character.* New York: St. Martin's Press.

Wilhelm, J. (1908). General Councils. *The Catholic Encyclopedia.* New York: Robert Appleton Company. Retrieved February 12, 2013 from: http://www.newadvent.org/cathen/04423f.htm

Wiltgen, R. M. (1985). *The Rhine flows into the Tiber*: A

history of Vatican II. Rockford, Illinois: Tan Books and Publishers, Inc.

Young, C. (2013, January) Putin goes to church: Russia's unholy new alliance between orthodox and state. *Reason Magazine*. Retrieved January 5, 2012 from: http://reason.com/archives/2012/12/26/putin-goes-to-church

Zwick, M. & L. (2005). *The Catholic worker movement: Intellectual and spiritual origins*. New York: Paulist Press.

About the Author

David H. Lukenbill is a former criminal—thief and robber—who has transformed his life through education—an Associate of Arts degree in Administration of Justice from Sacramento City College, a Bachelor of Science degree in Organizational Behavior from the University of San Francisco, and a Master of Public Administration degree from the University of San Francisco—several years developing, managing, and consulting with criminal transformative organizations, and a conversion to Catholicism.

He is married to his wife of 31 years and they have one child. They live by the American River in California with two cats, and all the wild critters they can feed.

Contact information at the Lampstand Foundation website www.lampstandfoundation.org

Prayer for Prisoners, Pope Pius XII

O Divine Prisoner of the sanctuary, Who for love of us and for our salvation not only enclosed Yourself within the narrow confines of human nature and then hid Yourself under the veils of the Sacramental Species, but also continually live in the tabernacle! Hear our prayer which rises to You from within these walls and which longs to express to You our affection, our sorrow, and the great need we have of You in our tribulations - above all, in the loss of freedom which so distresses us.

For some of us, there is probably a voice in the depths of conscience which says we are not guilty; that only a tragic judicial error has led us to this prison. In this case, we will draw comfort from remembering that You, the most August of all victims, were also condemned despite Your innocence.

Or perhaps, instead, we must lower our eyes to conceal our blush of shame, and beat our breast. But, even so, we also have the remedy of throwing ourselves into Your arms, certain that You understand all errors, forgive all sins, and generously restore Your grace to him who turns to You in repentance.

And finally, there are those among us who have succumbed to sin so often through the course of our earthly lives that even the best among men mistrust us, and we ourselves hardly know how to set out on the new road of regeneration. But despite all this, in the most hidden corner of our soul a voice of trust and comfort whispers Your words, promising us the help of Your light and Your grace if we want to return to what is good.

May we, o Lord, never forget that the day of trial is an opportune time for purifying the spirit, practicing the highest virtues, and acquiring the greatest merits. Let not our afflicted hearts be affected by that disgust which dries up everything, or by that distrust which leaves no room for brotherly sentiments and which prepared the road for bad counsel. May we always remember that, in depriving us of the freedom of our bodies, no one has been able to deprive us of freedom of the soul, which during the long hours of our solitude can rise to You to know You better and love You more each day.

Grant, o Divine Savior, help and resignation to the dear ones who mourn our absence. Grant peace and quiet to this world which has rejected us but which we love and to which we promise our co-operation as good citizens for the future.

Grant that our sorrows may be a salutary example to many souls and that they may thus be protected against the dangers of following our path. But above all, grant us the grace of believing firmly in You, of filially hoping in You, and of loving You: Who, with the Father and the Holy Spirit, live and reign forever and ever.

Amen.

O Sacred Heart of Jesus, make us love Thee more and more!
Our Lady of Hope, pray for us!
Saint Dismas, the Good Thief, pray for us!

Pius XII, April 1958

Prayer to St. Dismas

Glorious Saint Dismas, you alone of all the great Penitent Saints were directly canonized by Christ Himself; you were assured of a place in Heaven with Him "*this day*" because of the sincere confession of your sins to Him in the tribunal of Calvary and your true sorrow for them as you hung beside Him in that open confessional; you who by your love and repentance did open the Heart of Jesus in mercy and forgiveness even before the centurion's spear tore it asunder; you whose face was closer to that of Jesus in His last agony, to offer Him a word of comfort, closer even than that of His Beloved Mother, Mary; you who knew so well how to pray, teach me the words to say to Him to gain pardon and the grace of perseverance; and you who are so close to Him now in Heaven, as you were during His last moments on earth, pray to Him for me that I shall never again desert Him, but that at the close of my life I may hear from Him the words He addressed to you: "This day thou shalt be with Me in Paradise." Amen.

Prayer to St. Michael for Protection of the Catholic Church and Her Members

O Glorious St. Michael, Guardian and Defender of the Church of Jesus Christ, come to the assistance of the Church, against which the powers of Hell are unchained. Guard with thy special care her august visible head, and obtain for him and for us that the hour of triumph may speedily arrive.

O Glorious Archangel St. Michael, watch over us during life, defend us against the assaults of the demon, assist us especially at the hour of death, obtain for us a favorable judgment and the happiness of beholding God face to face for endless ages. Amen

www.ingramcontent.com/pod-product-compliance
Lightning Source LLC
La Vergne TN
LVHW051309080426
835509LV00020B/3192